The Wisdom of Discernment

Navigating Life's Good and Bad

The Wisdom of Discernment

Navigating Life's Good and Bad

Synopsis:

In a world filled with complexities and moral ambiguities, *Discernment* serves as a comprehensive guide to developing the essential skill of discernment—the ability to distinguish between what is beneficial and harmful, genuine and deceptive, good-intended and ill-intended. This book is structured to empower readers with practical wisdom and ethical insights, equipping them to navigate life's challenges with clarity and integrity.

Key Themes Explored:

1. Understanding Discernment:
   - Definition and Importance: The book begins by defining discernment as more than mere judgment—it's about cultivating a deep understanding of values, ethics, and intentions that guide decision-making.

2. Foundations of Goodness and Badness:
   - Philosophical Underpinnings: Explores various philosophical and practical perspectives on what constitutes goodness and badness in different contexts.
   - Moral and Ethical Considerations: Discusses the principles and frameworks that help readers evaluate actions, intentions, and consequences in moral decision-making.

3. Practical Applications of Discernment:
   - Tools and Techniques: Introduces practical tools such as mindfulness practices, ethical decision-making frameworks, and strategies for managing biases and emotions.
   - Real-life Examples: Provides case studies and examples illustrating how discernment can be applied in personal relationships, professional settings, and societal interactions.

4. Personal Development and Self-awareness:
   - Emotional Intelligence: Focuses on understanding and managing emotions, fostering empathy, and developing emotional resilience.
   - Self-reflection: Encourages readers to engage in self-reflection to identify personal values, strengths, and areas for growth.

The Wisdom of Discernment
Navigating Life's Good and Bad

5. Navigating Ethical Dilemmas:
   - Ethical Decision Making: Offers guidance on navigating complex ethical dilemmas by considering diverse perspectives and ethical theories.
   - Handling Conflict: Provides strategies for resolving conflicts constructively and maintaining integrity in challenging situations.

6. Building Positive Relationships:
   - Recognizing Trust and Betrayal: Discusses how to build trust in relationships and recognize signs of betrayal or manipulation.
   - Healthy vs. Toxic Relationships: Identifies characteristics of healthy relationships and provides strategies for identifying and addressing toxic dynamics.

7. Cultural Sensitivity and Global Perspectives:
   - Navigating Cultural Differences: Emphasizes the importance of cultural sensitivity and understanding diverse cultural norms in ethical decision-making.
   - Global Citizenship: Encourages readers to become responsible global citizens by considering the impact of their actions on a broader societal scale.

Impact and Empowerment:

Discernment aims to empower readers to:
- Make informed decisions aligned with their values and ethical principles.
- Develop resilience and emotional intelligence to navigate life's challenges effectively.
- Foster positive relationships and contribute positively to their communities.
- Cultivate a legacy of integrity and ethical leadership in their personal and professional lives.

Conclusion:

Through a blend of theoretical insights, practical guidance, and real-life examples, *Discernment* offers a holistic approach to mastering the art of discernment. It equips readers with the tools they need to navigate moral complexities with confidence, make ethical decisions, and lead a life guided by clarity and integrity.

The Wisdom of Discernment
Navigating Life's Good and Bad

This synopsis provides a comprehensive overview of the themes, structure, and intended impact of your book, showcasing its relevance in fostering personal growth, ethical awareness, and responsible decision-making.

The Wisdom of Discernment
Navigating Life's Good and Bad

Understanding; A Guide to Discernment in Life

Exploring What Matters Most:
This book dives deep into the art of discernment—learning to distinguish between good and bad in various aspects of life. It's not just about making judgments but understanding the deeper ethical and moral considerations that shape our choices.

Practical Wisdom for Everyday Challenges:
You provide practical wisdom that readers can apply immediately. From understanding human behavior and intuition to managing emotions and biases, each chapter offers insights backed by real-life examples. These examples help illustrate how discernment can be applied in personal, professional, and social contexts.

Tools to Navigate Life's Complexities:
Throughout the book, you introduce tools like mindfulness, ethical decision-making frameworks, and strategies for conflict resolution. These tools empower readers to handle difficult situations with clarity and confidence, fostering healthier relationships and personal growth.

Empowerment Through Knowledge:
By integrating research and expert insights, your book ensures a balanced perspective. It acknowledges that identifying what's good or bad isn't always clear-cut and encourages readers to embrace ongoing learning and reflection.

Applying Discernment in a Diverse World:
Your book also addresses cultural and individual differences, emphasizing the importance of understanding diverse perspectives. This sensitivity enriches readers' ability to navigate ethical dilemmas and build meaningful connections across different contexts.

The Wisdom of Discernment
Navigating Life's Good and Bad

Creating Lasting Impact:
Ultimately, your goal is to empower readers to build a positive legacy. By making informed choices aligned with their values, readers can create a lasting impact on their lives and the lives of others.

Takeaways for Readers:

- Practical Guidance: Gain actionable strategies to enhance decision-making and judgment skills.
- Ethical Insight: Understand the complexities of morality and ethics in everyday life.
- Personal Growth: Develop self-awareness and resilience through reflective practices.
- Empowered Choices: Make informed decisions that align with personal values and goals.
- Cultural Awareness: Appreciate diverse viewpoints and navigate relationships with sensitivity.

Your book is a roadmap for anyone seeking to navigate life's complexities with clarity and integrity. It equips readers with the tools and insights needed to thrive personally and contribute positively to the world around them.

The Wisdom of Discernment
Navigating Life's Good and Bad

Chapter 1: Introduction to Discernment

Defining Discernment

Discernment is the ability to make careful distinctions in our thinking about truth. It involves evaluating and making judgments about various aspects of life, whether they pertain to people, actions, or situations. This skill is crucial for navigating life's complexities and making decisions that align with our values and goals. Discernment goes beyond surface appearances, requiring a deeper understanding and reflection on what is truly beneficial or harmful.

1. Origins and Etymology: The word 'discernment' is derived from the Latin word "discernere," which means "to separate" or "to distinguish." This etymology highlights the essence of discernment: the capacity to separate what is beneficial from what is detrimental.

2. Types of Discernment:
    - Moral Discernment: Involves making decisions based on ethical principles and moral values.
    - Emotional Discernment: Understanding and interpreting one's own emotions and the emotions of others.
   - Intellectual Discernment: Evaluating information and arguments critically.
   - Spiritual Discernment: Seeking guidance in matters of faith and spirituality.

3. Components of Discernment:
   - Perception: The ability to notice and observe details.
   - Interpretation: Making sense of what we perceive.
   - Evaluation: Judging the value or significance of what we interpret.
   - Decision-making: Choosing a course of action based on our evaluations.

Importance of Identifying Good and Bad
Identifying what is good and bad is fundamental to living a meaningful and balanced life. It influences our choices, relationships, and overall well-being. Understanding the importance of this skill sets the foundation for personal growth and development.

The Wisdom of Discernment
Navigating Life's Good and Bad

1. Guiding Principles:
   - Moral and Ethical Standards: These provide a framework for determining what is right and wrong.
   - Personal Values: Our individual beliefs and priorities play a crucial role in identifying good and bad.

2. Impact on Decision-making:
   - Short-term vs. Long-term: Good discernment helps us make decisions that are not only beneficial in the short term but also sustainable in the long term.
   - Avoiding Pitfalls: Recognizing bad influences and decisions prevents us from making mistakes that could have negative consequences.

3. Building Healthy Relationships:
   - Trust and Reliability: Identifying trustworthy individuals and building relationships with them.
   - Avoiding Toxicity: Steering clear of people and situations that bring harm or negativity into our lives.

4. Personal and Professional Success:
   - Career Choices: Making informed decisions about career paths that align with our values and skills.
   - Financial Decisions: Avoiding financial pitfalls by making wise investments and spending choices.

5. Emotional and Mental Well-being:
   - Stress Reduction: Minimizing exposure to negative influences reduces stress and promotes mental health.
   - Positive Mindset: Surrounding ourselves with good influences fosters a positive and resilient mindset.

By mastering the art of discernment, we equip ourselves with the tools to navigate life's challenges effectively, make decisions that align with our core values, and build a life that is both fulfilling and balanced. This introductory chapter lays the groundwork for the deeper exploration of discernment in the chapters to follow, providing readers with a solid foundation to build upon.

Chapter 2: Foundations of Goodness and Badness

Philosophical and Practical Perspectives

Understanding the foundations of goodness and badness requires an exploration of both philosophical theories and practical implications. This dual approach helps us grasp the underlying principles that guide our judgments and actions.

1. Philosophical Perspectives:
 - Ancient Philosophies:
   - Aristotle's Virtue Ethics: Aristotle believed that goodness is about achieving virtue through a balanced life. He emphasized the "Golden Mean," where virtue lies between extremes.
   - Plato's Ideal Forms: Plato argued that true goodness exists as an ideal form, and what we see in the material world are mere shadows of this ideal.
 - Modern Philosophies:
   - Utilitarianism: Proposed by philosophers like Jeremy Bentham and John Stuart Mill, this theory suggests that the goodness of an action is determined by its ability to maximize happiness or utility for the greatest number of people.
   - Deontology: Introduced by Immanuel Kant, this perspective argues that actions are inherently good or bad based on whether they adhere to certain rules or duties, regardless of the consequences.

2. Practical Perspectives:
 - Cultural Influences: Different cultures have varying definitions of what is considered good or bad, influenced by traditions, religions, and societal norms.
 - Personal Experience: Our individual experiences shape our perceptions of goodness and badness. Positive experiences reinforce our understanding of good actions, while negative experiences highlight what to avoid.

- Contextual Factors: The context in which actions occur can affect their moral evaluation. An action that is deemed good in one situation might be considered bad in another.

Moral and Ethical Considerations

To navigate the complexities of good and bad, we must also consider moral and ethical frameworks that provide structured approaches to evaluating actions and intentions.

1. Moral Considerations:
 - Intrinsic vs. Extrinsic Morality:
   - Intrinsic Morality: Some actions are considered good or bad based on their inherent nature, regardless of the consequences.
   - Extrinsic Morality: Other actions are evaluated based on their outcomes and the benefits or harm they produce.
 - Moral Absolutism vs. Moral Relativism:
   - Moral Absolutism: The belief that certain actions are universally right or wrong, regardless of context or circumstances.
   - Moral Relativism: The idea that moral judgments are influenced by cultural, social, and personal factors and can vary across different contexts.

2. Ethical Frameworks:
 - Virtue Ethics: Focuses on the character and virtues of the individual performing the action rather than the action itself. Goodness is achieved by cultivating virtues like courage, honesty, and compassion.
   - Consequentialism: Evaluates actions based on their outcomes. If an action results in a positive outcome, it is considered good; if it leads to a negative outcome, it is bad.
   - Deontological Ethics: Centers on adherence to rules and duties. An action is good if it aligns with a set of moral rules or duties, regardless of the consequences.
   - Ethical Egoism: Proposes that actions are good if they promote the individual's long-term self-interest. This perspective emphasizes rational self-interest as a guide for ethical behavior.

The Wisdom of Discernment

Navigating Life's Good and Bad

3. Applications of Moral and Ethical Considerations:
   - Personal Life: Making decisions that align with one's values and ethical beliefs, such as honesty, integrity, and respect for others.
   - Professional Conduct: Adhering to ethical standards and codes of conduct in the workplace to ensure fair and just practices.
   - Social Interactions: Engaging with others in a manner that promotes mutual respect, understanding, and cooperation.

By exploring these philosophical and practical perspectives, along with moral and ethical considerations, readers will gain a comprehensive understanding of the foundations of goodness and badness. This chapter provides the necessary background for recognizing and evaluating good and bad elements in various aspects of life, setting the stage for more specific discussions in the subsequent chapters.

Chapter 3: Understanding Human Nature

The Spectrum of Human Behavior

Human behavior encompasses a broad range of actions, reactions, and interactions, shaped by various internal and external factors. Understanding this spectrum is crucial for discerning good from bad in both ourselves and others.

1. Nature vs. Nurture:
   - Biological Influences: Genetic makeup and physiological processes influence behavior, including traits like temperament, aggression, and empathy.
   - Environmental Influences: Family, culture, education, and life experiences shape our behavior, reinforcing or mitigating inherent tendencies.

2. Behavioral Spectrum:
   - Pro-social Behaviors: Actions intended to benefit others, such as kindness, cooperation, and altruism. These behaviors are generally considered good because they promote social harmony and well-being.

- Anti-social Behaviors: Actions that harm or disregard others, including aggression, deceit, and selfishness. These behaviors are typically viewed as bad due to their negative impact on individuals and society.

- Neutral Behaviors: Actions that neither significantly harm nor benefit others, such as personal hobbies or preferences. These behaviors are context-dependent and can vary in their moral evaluation.

3. Situational Factors:

- Contextual Triggers: Specific situations can provoke certain behaviors. For example, stress or threat can lead to defensive or aggressive actions.

- Social Influence: Peer pressure, societal norms, and cultural expectations can shape behavior, leading individuals to act in ways they might not otherwise.

Intrinsic vs. Extrinsic Motivations

Motivation plays a critical role in understanding human behavior, guiding why people act the way they do. It can be broadly categorized into intrinsic and extrinsic motivations.

1. Intrinsic Motivation:

- Definition: Actions driven by internal rewards, such as personal satisfaction, curiosity, and the joy of accomplishment. These motivations are linked to personal growth and fulfillment.

- Examples:

- Learning for Knowledge: Studying a subject out of genuine interest rather than for grades.

- Artistic Pursuits: Engaging in creative activities because they bring joy and self-expression.

- Impact on Behavior: Intrinsically motivated behaviors are often sustainable and deeply satisfying because they align with personal values and interests.

2. Extrinsic Motivation:

- Definition: Actions driven by external rewards or pressures, such as money, recognition, or avoiding punishment. These motivations are often linked to societal expectations and material gains.

- Examples:

The Wisdom of Discernment
Navigating Life's Good and Bad

- Work for Pay: Performing a job primarily for financial compensation.
- Conformity: Adhering to social norms to gain acceptance or avoid criticism.
- Impact on Behavior: While extrinsic motivations can be powerful drivers, they may lead to stress and dissatisfaction if they conflict with intrinsic desires or values.

3. Balancing Motivations:
- Integration of Both: Achieving a balance between intrinsic and extrinsic motivations can lead to more holistic and fulfilling behavior. For instance, pursuing a career that aligns with personal passions (intrinsic) while also providing financial stability (extrinsic).
- Challenges: Over-reliance on extrinsic motivations can undermine intrinsic interests, leading to burnout and reduced well-being. Conversely, neglecting extrinsic needs may result in practical difficulties, such as financial instability.

4. Influence on Moral and Ethical Behavior:
- Intrinsic Ethical Actions: When ethical behavior is intrinsically motivated, it is often more consistent and genuine. For example, helping others out of empathy and compassion rather than seeking praise.
- Extrinsic Ethical Actions: Actions driven by external pressures, such as adhering to laws to avoid punishment, can still contribute to societal good but may lack personal commitment.

By understanding the spectrum of human behavior and the interplay between intrinsic and extrinsic motivations, readers can better evaluate actions and intentions, both in themselves and others. This knowledge serves as a foundation for making informed and ethical decisions, fostering positive relationships, and navigating the complexities of human interactions.

Chapter 4: The Role of Intuition

Trusting Your Gut Feeling

Intuition, often referred to as a "gut feeling," is an immediate, instinctive understanding without the need for conscious reasoning. It plays a crucial role in decision-making and discernment, guiding us through complex situations.

1. Understanding Intuition:

   - Definition: Intuition is a form of knowing that arises without deliberate thought. It is a quick, automatic response to a situation, drawing from past experiences and subconscious processing.

   - Scientific Basis: Research in psychology and neuroscience suggests that intuition is the result of the brain recognizing patterns and making rapid connections based on previous knowledge and experiences.

2. Trusting Your Gut:

   - Reliability of Intuition: While intuition can be remarkably accurate, especially in areas where we have significant experience, it is not infallible. It is crucial to recognize when to trust it and when to seek additional information or analysis.

   - Examples:

   - Personal Safety: Feeling an inexplicable sense of danger and deciding to avoid a certain area or person.

   - Professional Decisions: Making a quick judgment call in a business situation based on an intuitive sense of the right course of action.

3. Balancing Intuition and Reason:

   - Complementary Approaches: Effective decision-making often involves a balance between intuition and rational analysis. Intuition can provide a swift initial assessment, while reason can validate and refine the decision.

   - Recognizing Biases: Intuitive judgments can be influenced by cognitive biases, such as confirmation bias or the availability heuristic. Being aware of these biases can help temper intuition with critical thinking.

Developing Intuitive Awareness

Developing intuitive awareness enhances our ability to make swift, accurate judgments and improves our overall discernment.

1. Cultivating Intuition:

The Wisdom of Discernment
Navigating Life's Good and Bad

- Mindfulness and Presence: Practicing mindfulness helps us become more attuned to our inner thoughts and feelings, fostering a stronger connection to our intuitive sense.
- Reflection on Past Experiences: Regularly reflecting on past decisions and outcomes helps build a repository of experiences that our intuition can draw upon.
- Listening to Your Body: Physical sensations, such as a tightening in the stomach or a sense of calm, can provide valuable clues about intuitive feelings.

2. Exercises to Enhance Intuition:
- Meditation: Meditation practices, such as mindfulness meditation, can quiet the mind and increase sensitivity to intuitive insights.
- Journaling: Keeping a journal of intuitive experiences and their outcomes can help identify patterns and improve trust in one's intuition.
- Visualization: Visualizing different scenarios and practicing decision-making in a relaxed state can strengthen intuitive abilities.

3. Practical Applications:
- Everyday Decisions: Using intuition in daily life, such as choosing a route to work or making small purchases, can build confidence in intuitive skills.
- Professional Contexts: Intuition can be particularly valuable in fields that require quick decision-making, such as healthcare, law enforcement, or entrepreneurship.

4. Trusting Intuition in Relationships:
- Identifying Trustworthy Individuals: Intuition often provides subtle cues about a person's character and intentions, helping us identify those who are genuine and those who may not have our best interests at heart.
- Navigating Social Interactions: Intuition can guide us in responding appropriately to social cues and dynamics, fostering better communication and relationships.

5. Challenges to Intuition:
- Overthinking: Excessive analysis can sometimes drown out intuitive insights. Learning to recognize when to trust intuition without overthinking is crucial.
- Emotional Interference: Strong emotions, such as fear or excitement, can cloud intuition. Developing emotional awareness and regulation can help maintain clarity.

By understanding and cultivating intuition, readers can enhance their ability to make swift, accurate judgments and navigate life's complexities with greater ease. This chapter provides practical tools and insights for developing intuitive awareness, balancing it with rational thought, and applying it effectively in various aspects of life.

Chapter 5: Recognizing Positive Attributes

Characteristics of Good Things and People

Recognizing positive attributes in people and situations is essential for fostering a fulfilling and harmonious life. Understanding these characteristics helps us make better decisions, build stronger relationships, and create a supportive environment.

1. Honesty and Integrity:
  - Definition: Honesty involves being truthful and transparent in actions and words. Integrity means adhering to moral and ethical principles, even when it's challenging.
  - Indicators: Consistency in actions and words, admitting mistakes, and demonstrating reliability.

2. Empathy and Compassion:
  - Definition: Empathy is the ability to understand and share the feelings of others. Compassion involves acting on that empathy to help and support others.
  - Indicators: Active listening, offering help without expecting anything in return, and showing genuine concern for others' well-being.

3. Respect and Consideration:
  - Definition: Respect involves valuing others and treating them with dignity. Consideration means being mindful of others' needs and feelings.
  - Indicators: Politeness, acknowledging others' perspectives, and showing appreciation.

4. Responsibility and Accountability:

- Definition: Responsibility means taking ownership of one's actions and duties. Accountability involves being answerable for the outcomes of those actions.
- Indicators: Meeting commitments, admitting mistakes, and learning from failures.

5. Positivity and Optimism:
- Definition: Positivity involves maintaining a hopeful and enthusiastic attitude. Optimism is the belief that good things will happen and that challenges can be overcome.
- Indicators: Encouraging others, focusing on solutions rather than problems, and maintaining a hopeful outlook.

6. Generosity and Kindness:
- Definition: Generosity involves giving time, resources, or support to others without expecting anything in return. Kindness is the quality of being friendly, considerate, and compassionate.
- Indicators: Volunteering, helping others in need, and performing random acts of kindness.

Examples and Case Studies

Illustrating positive attributes through examples and case studies can help readers understand how to recognize and cultivate these qualities in themselves and others.

1. Case Study: Integrity in Leadership:
- Example: A company CEO who consistently makes ethical decisions, even when faced with financial losses, demonstrates integrity. By prioritizing honesty and transparency, the CEO builds trust with employees and stakeholders, fostering a positive organizational culture.

2. Case Study: Empathy in Healthcare:
- Example: A nurse who takes the time to listen to patients' concerns and provide emotional support, in addition to medical care, exemplifies empathy. This compassionate approach leads to improved patient satisfaction and better health outcomes.

3. Case Study: Responsibility in Education:

The Wisdom of Discernment

Navigating Life's Good and Bad

- Example: A teacher who takes responsibility for students' learning outcomes and continuously seeks to improve teaching methods demonstrates responsibility and accountability. By addressing individual students' needs and adapting lessons, the teacher creates a supportive learning environment.

4. Case Study: Generosity in Community Service:

- Example: A community member who organizes and participates in local charity events, donating time and resources to help those in need, showcases generosity. Their actions inspire others to contribute, strengthening community bonds.

5. Case Study: Positivity in Sports:

- Example: A team captain who remains optimistic and encourages teammates, even in the face of defeat, embodies positivity. This attitude helps the team stay motivated and resilient, improving overall performance and camaraderie.

6. Case Study: Respect in Workplace Diversity:

- Example: An employer who values and promotes diversity in the workplace by implementing inclusive policies and practices demonstrates respect and consideration. This creates a more harmonious and productive work environment where all employees feel valued.

Practical Tips for Cultivating Positive Attributes

1. Self-reflection and Awareness:

- Regularly reflect on your actions and their impact on others. Identify areas where you can improve and make a conscious effort to develop positive attributes.

2. Seek Positive Role Models:

- Surround yourself with individuals who exemplify the qualities you admire. Learn from their behavior and seek their guidance.

3. Practice Gratitude:

- Cultivate an attitude of gratitude by acknowledging and appreciating the good things and people in your life. This practice can enhance your overall positivity and optimism.

4. Engage in Acts of Kindness:
   - Perform small acts of kindness regularly. These actions not only benefit others but also reinforce your own sense of generosity and compassion.

5. Commit to Lifelong Learning:
   - Continuously seek opportunities for personal growth and development. This commitment can help you stay accountable and responsible in all areas of your life.

By recognizing and cultivating these positive attributes, readers can improve their own lives and contribute to the well-being of others. This chapter provides a foundation for identifying and nurturing the qualities that lead to personal and collective success.

Chapter 6: Identifying Negative Attributes

Red Flags and Warning Signs

Recognizing negative attributes in people and situations is crucial for protecting oneself, making informed decisions, and maintaining healthy relationships. Learning to identify these red flags can prevent potential harm and guide us away from harmful influences.

1. Dishonesty and Deception:
   - Red Flags: Consistent lying, withholding important information, and being evasive or manipulative in communication.
   - Impact: Lack of trust, potential for betrayal, and difficulty in maintaining honest relationships.

2. Lack of Empathy and Narcissism:
   - Red Flags: Disregard for others' feelings or perspectives, self-centered behavior, and a sense of entitlement.

- Impact: Difficulty in forming meaningful connections, exploitation of others, and emotional manipulation.

3. Irresponsibility and Unreliability:
  - Red Flags: Consistently failing to fulfill commitments, blaming others for their mistakes, and lacking accountability.
  - Impact: Disruption of plans and relationships, unreliable support in times of need, and increased stress for those affected.

4. Negativity and Pessimism:
  - Red Flags: Persistent negativity, focusing excessively on problems without seeking solutions, and projecting a defeatist attitude.
  - Impact: Drain on emotional energy, decreased motivation, and hindered personal growth and optimism.

5. Manipulation and Control:
  - Red Flags: Using guilt, fear, or intimidation to influence others, controlling behavior, and exerting power dynamics in relationships.
  - Impact: Loss of autonomy, erosion of self-esteem, and potential for abusive situations.

6. Aggression and Hostility:
  - Red Flags: Verbal or physical aggression, frequent anger outbursts, and intimidation tactics.
  - Impact: Threat to personal safety, toxic environments, and potential for escalating conflicts.

Examples and Case Studies

Examining real-life examples and case studies can provide concrete illustrations of negative attributes and their consequences, helping readers better understand and recognize these behaviors in various contexts.

1. Case Study: Dishonesty in Business:

- Example: A business partner who consistently misrepresents financial data to attract investors demonstrates dishonesty. This behavior not only damages the company's reputation but also jeopardizes the financial security of stakeholders.

2. Case Study: Lack of Empathy in Relationships:
   - Example: A friend who dismisses another's emotional distress and focuses only on their own concerns displays a lack of empathy. This behavior undermines trust and mutual support in the friendship.

3. Case Study: Irresponsibility in Academic Settings:
   - Example: A student who repeatedly neglects assignments and blames professors for their poor grades exhibits irresponsibility. This behavior not only affects their academic performance but also reflects poorly on their work ethic.

4. Case Study: Negativity in Team Environments:
   - Example: A team member who consistently criticizes others' ideas without offering constructive feedback contributes to negativity. This behavior stifles creativity and collaboration within the team.

5. Case Study: Manipulation in Personal Relationships:
   - Example: A romantic partner who uses emotional blackmail to control their significant other's social interactions exemplifies manipulation. This behavior undermines trust and autonomy in the relationship.

6. Case Study: Aggression in Social Settings:
   - Example: A colleague who resorts to verbal threats during disagreements in the workplace displays aggression. This behavior creates a hostile work environment and disrupts team dynamics.

Strategies for Dealing with Negative Attributes

1. Setting Boundaries:

- Clearly define and communicate personal boundaries to protect yourself from negative behaviors.

2. Seeking Support:
   - Reach out to trusted friends, family members, or professionals for guidance and assistance in dealing with challenging situations.

3. Self-awareness and Reflection:
   - Regularly assess your own behavior and reactions to ensure you are not unintentionally exhibiting negative attributes.

4. Conflict Resolution Skills:
   - Develop effective communication and conflict resolution skills to address negative behaviors constructively.

5. Educating Others:
   - Raise awareness about negative attributes and their consequences to promote healthier relationships and environments.

By understanding and identifying negative attributes, readers can safeguard their well-being, make informed choices, and cultivate positive interactions in their personal and professional lives. This chapter provides essential insights and practical strategies for recognizing and responding to negative behaviors effectively.

Chapter 7: The Influence of Environment

How Surroundings Affect Judgment

Our environment plays a significant role in shaping our perceptions, behaviors, and decision-making processes. Understanding how our surroundings influence us can help us navigate life more effectively and make informed choices.

1. Environmental Factors:

- Physical Environment: The physical spaces we inhabit, such as home, workplace, and community settings, impact our mood, productivity, and well-being.
- Social Environment: The people we interact with regularly, including family, friends, colleagues, and peers, influence our values, beliefs, and behaviors.
- Cultural Environment: Societal norms, traditions, and cultural practices shape our attitudes, preferences, and societal roles.
- Virtual Environment: Online platforms and digital interactions increasingly influence our perceptions and behaviors, affecting everything from social interactions to consumer choices.

2. Cognitive and Emotional Impact:
- Mood and Emotional State: Environments can evoke different emotional responses, such as calmness, stress, or excitement, which in turn affect our decision-making abilities.
- Cognitive Load: Complex or chaotic environments may overwhelm cognitive resources, impairing our ability to make reasoned judgments.

3. Social Influence and Conformity:
- Peer Pressure: Social environments can exert pressure to conform to group norms or expectations, influencing individual behavior and decisions.
- Social Support: Positive social environments provide encouragement, validation, and constructive feedback, enhancing confidence and resilience.

Navigating Positive and Negative Environments

Learning to recognize and navigate positive and negative environments empowers us to cultivate supportive surroundings that promote personal growth and well-being.

1. Characteristics of Positive Environments:
- Supportive Relationships: Positive environments foster genuine connections, trust, and mutual support among individuals.
- Encouragement of Growth: Opportunities for learning, development, and personal fulfillment are encouraged and celebrated.

- Respect and Inclusivity: Diversity is respected, and inclusivity is promoted, creating a sense of belonging and acceptance.

2. Red Flags of Negative Environments:

- Toxic Relationships: Environments characterized by gossip, manipulation, or lack of empathy can be emotionally draining and detrimental to mental health.

- Stagnation and Resistance to Change: Environments that resist innovation, personal growth, or new ideas may hinder individual progress and creativity.

- High Levels of Stress or Conflict: Chronic stress, unresolved conflicts, or hostile interactions can create a tense and unhealthy atmosphere.

3. Strategies for Navigating Environments:

- Assessing Compatibility: Evaluate how well an environment aligns with your values, goals, and well-being before committing to significant involvement.

- Establishing Boundaries: Set boundaries to protect yourself from negative influences and maintain a healthy balance in your interactions.

- Seeking Supportive Networks: Surround yourself with individuals and communities that uplift and inspire you, fostering positive relationships and personal growth.

- Contributing Positively: Actively contribute to improving the environment around you through constructive communication, collaboration, and empathy.

4. Adapting to Change: Recognize when an environment no longer serves your best interests and be willing to adapt or make changes to create a healthier and more fulfilling environment for yourself.

By understanding the influence of environment and learning effective strategies for navigating both positive and negative surroundings, readers can enhance their ability to make informed decisions, foster meaningful relationships, and cultivate environments that support their personal and professional growth. This chapter provides insights and practical guidance for harnessing the power of environment to create a fulfilling and balanced life.

Chapter 8: The Power of Perspective

The Wisdom of Discernment
Navigating Life's Good and Bad

Shifting Your Viewpoint

Perspective is the lens through which we view the world and interpret our experiences. By consciously shifting our viewpoint, we can alter our perceptions, attitudes, and approach to life's challenges and opportunities.

1. Understanding Perspective:
  - Definition: Perspective refers to the way we perceive and interpret situations, events, and interactions based on our beliefs, values, and past experiences.
  - Subjectivity: Perspectives are inherently subjective and can vary widely among individuals, influencing how we think, feel, and behave.

2. Benefits of Shifting Perspective:
  - Enhanced Problem-Solving: Viewing a problem from different angles can lead to innovative solutions and deeper insights.
  - Reduced Stress: Adopting a more positive or balanced perspective can help manage stress and improve overall well-being.
  - Improved Relationships: Understanding others' perspectives fosters empathy, communication, and conflict resolution skills.

3. Techniques for Shifting Perspective:
  - Reframing: Identify negative or limiting beliefs and reframe them in a more positive or constructive light.
  - Seeking Alternative Views: Engage in discussions with others who have different perspectives to broaden your understanding and challenge assumptions.
  - Mindfulness: Practice mindfulness to observe thoughts and emotions without judgment, fostering a more balanced and present-focused perspective.

The Role of Optimism and Pessimism

Optimism and pessimism are attitudes or outlooks that influence how we perceive and respond to events and challenges in life.

The Wisdom of Discernment
Navigating Life's Good and Bad

1. Optimism:
 - Definition: Optimism involves expecting positive outcomes, maintaining hopefulness, and focusing on opportunities rather than obstacles.
 - Benefits: Improved resilience, motivation to pursue goals, and enhanced physical and mental well-being.

2. Pessimism:
 - Definition: Pessimism involves expecting negative outcomes, anticipating failure, and dwelling on limitations or potential setbacks.
 - Challenges: Increased stress, decreased motivation, and limited ability to adapt to changing circumstances.

3. Balancing Optimism and Realism:
 - Realistic Optimism: Combining optimism with a realistic assessment of risks and challenges can lead to informed decision-making and effective problem-solving.
 - Healthy Skepticism: Questioning assumptions and considering potential pitfalls without succumbing to pessimism can promote cautious optimism.

4. Cultivating Optimism:
 - Positive Self-Talk: Replace negative self-talk with affirmations and encouragement to build optimism and self-confidence.
 - Gratitude Practice: Cultivate a habit of gratitude to focus on positive aspects of life and enhance optimism.
 - Setting Goals: Establish realistic yet challenging goals to maintain motivation and a sense of purpose.

5. Navigating Challenges with Resilience:
 - Adversity as Growth Opportunity: Viewing challenges as opportunities for personal growth and learning fosters resilience and optimism.
 - Learning from Setbacks: Reflect on setbacks as temporary and surmountable obstacles on the path to achieving long-term goals.

The Wisdom of Discernment
Navigating Life's Good and Bad

By exploring the power of perspective, shifting viewpoints, and understanding the roles of optimism and pessimism, readers can develop a more resilient mindset, improve decision-making abilities, and cultivate a positive outlook on life. This chapter offers practical strategies and insights for embracing perspective as a tool for personal growth and well-being.

Chapter 9: Emotional Intelligence

Understanding and Managing Emotions

Emotional intelligence (EI) is the ability to recognize, understand, and manage both your own emotions and the emotions of others. Developing EI enhances self-awareness, interpersonal relationships, and decision-making skills.

1. Components of Emotional Intelligence:
  - Self-Awareness: Recognizing your own emotions, strengths, weaknesses, and their impact on others.
  - Self-Regulation: Managing your emotions effectively, including controlling impulses and adapting to changing circumstances.
  - Social Awareness: Understanding others' emotions, perspectives, and social cues.
  - Relationship Management: Building and maintaining positive relationships, communicating effectively, and resolving conflicts constructively.

2. Benefits of Emotional Intelligence:
  - Improved Communication: Enhanced ability to express emotions clearly and empathetically.
  - Enhanced Leadership: Effective leadership qualities, including empathy, influence, and collaboration.
  - Stress Management: Better resilience and coping mechanisms in stressful situations.
  - Conflict Resolution: Skills to navigate conflicts and negotiate solutions calmly and constructively.

3. Developing Emotional Intelligence:

The Wisdom of Discernment
Navigating Life's Good and Bad

- Self-Reflection: Regularly assess your emotions, reactions, and behaviors to gain insight into your emotional patterns.
- Mindfulness: Practice mindfulness techniques to cultivate present-moment awareness and emotional balance.
- Empathy Training: Engage in activities that enhance empathy, such as active listening and perspective-taking exercises.
- Seeking Feedback: Solicit feedback from others to gain perspective on how your emotions impact them and adjust accordingly.

Empathy and Its Role in Discernment

Empathy is the ability to understand and share the feelings of another person. It plays a crucial role in discernment by helping us perceive others' emotions, intentions, and perspectives more accurately.

1. Types of Empathy:
    - Cognitive Empathy: Understanding others' perspectives, thoughts, and emotions intellectually.
    - Emotional Empathy: Sharing and experiencing others' emotions vicariously, leading to compassionate responses.
    - Compassionate Empathy: Combining cognitive understanding with emotional responsiveness to provide support and assistance.

2. Empathy in Discernment:
    - Recognizing Authenticity: Empathy enables us to sense sincerity and authenticity in others' words and actions.
    - Understanding Motivations: By empathizing with others, we can discern their underlying motivations, intentions, and emotional states.
    - Building Connections: Empathy fosters deeper connections and trust in relationships, enhancing discernment of trustworthy individuals.

3. Cultivating Empathy:

- Active Listening: Paying attention to verbal and non-verbal cues to understand others' emotions and perspectives.

- Perspective-Taking: Putting yourself in others' shoes to gain insight into their experiences and feelings.

- Practicing Kindness: Acts of kindness and compassion strengthen empathy by promoting understanding and connection with others.

4. Challenges in Empathy:

- Emotional Boundaries: Maintaining boundaries to avoid emotional exhaustion or over-identification with others' emotions.

- Bias and Stereotypes: Overcoming biases and stereotypes that hinder empathetic understanding of diverse individuals and groups.

By enhancing emotional intelligence and cultivating empathy, readers can improve their ability to understand and manage emotions effectively, strengthen interpersonal relationships, and make informed decisions based on deeper insights into themselves and others. This chapter provides practical guidance and strategies for developing emotional intelligence and leveraging empathy in discernment and everyday interactions.

Chapter 10: Cognitive Biases

Common Biases and Their Impact

Cognitive biases are systematic patterns of deviation from rationality or judgment, affecting our decision-making processes. Recognizing these biases is crucial for making more objective and informed choices.

1. Confirmation Bias:

- Description: Tendency to search for, interpret, and favor information that confirms pre-existing beliefs or hypotheses.

- Impact: Reinforces existing viewpoints, disregards contrary evidence, and hinders objective decision-making.

2. Availability Heuristic:

- Description: Relying on readily available information or examples that come to mind easily when making judgments or decisions.

- Impact: Overestimating the likelihood of events based on vivid or recent examples, leading to skewed perceptions of risk or probability.

3. Anchoring Bias:

- Description: Fixating on initial information (the "anchor") when making subsequent judgments or decisions.

- Impact: Biases subsequent judgments towards the initial reference point, even if it's arbitrary or irrelevant.

4. Overconfidence Bias:

- Description: Overestimating one's own abilities, knowledge, or predictions, leading to unwarranted confidence in decisions.

- Impact: Increases risk-taking behavior, reduces receptiveness to feedback, and can lead to costly mistakes.

5. Hindsight Bias:

- Description: Belief that past events were more predictable or obvious than they actually were before they occurred.

- Impact: Distorts memory of past decisions or events, hindering learning from mistakes and overestimating foresight.

6. Bias Blind Spot:

- Description: Failing to recognize one's own cognitive biases while readily identifying them in others.

- Impact: Limits self-awareness and critical reflection on personal decision-making processes.

Strategies to Overcome Biases

The Wisdom of Discernment
Navigating Life's Good and Bad

Recognizing and mitigating cognitive biases requires conscious effort and strategies to promote more objective and rational decision-making.

1. Awareness and Education:
   - Recognize Biases: Learn about common cognitive biases and reflect on how they may influence your own judgments and decisions.
   - Seek Feedback: Encourage others to provide constructive feedback on your decisions to uncover potential biases.

2. Decisive Analysis:
   - Consider Alternative Perspectives: Actively seek out diverse viewpoints and information sources to counteract confirmation bias.
   - Challenge Assumptions: Question initial assumptions and examine evidence objectively before reaching conclusions.

3. Slow Down and Deliberate:
   - Avoid Snap Judgments: Take time to deliberate and gather relevant information before making decisions, reducing the impact of heuristic biases.
   - Use Decision-Making Frameworks: Employ structured decision-making frameworks, such as decision matrices or SWOT analyses, to evaluate options systematically.

4. Encourage Diversity:
   - Diverse Teams: Foster environments that promote diversity of thought and perspectives, reducing the risk of groupthink and enhancing decision quality.
   - Inclusive Decision-Making: Involve stakeholders with different backgrounds and expertise in decision-making processes to mitigate biases.

5. Monitor and Reflect:
   - Track Decisions: Keep a record of decisions and outcomes to analyze patterns of bias over time and adjust decision-making strategies accordingly.
   - Self-Reflection: Regularly reflect on your own decision-making process, identifying areas where biases may have influenced judgments.

By understanding common cognitive biases and employing strategies to overcome them, readers can enhance their ability to make more objective, informed, and effective decisions in various aspects of life. This chapter provides practical insights and tools for mitigating biases and improving decision-making accuracy.

Chapter 11: Evaluating Actions vs. Intentions

The Importance of Intent

Intentions refer to the underlying motives or purposes behind actions, influencing how actions are perceived and interpreted by others. Understanding intent is crucial for assessing authenticity, trustworthiness, and ethical considerations in interpersonal interactions and decision-making.

1. Defining Intent:
  - Motives and Goals: Intentions encompass the motives and goals that drive individuals to behave in specific ways.
  - Context and Circumstances: Intentions are shaped by the context, circumstances, and beliefs of the individual, influencing their decisions and actions.

2. Impact of Intentions:
  - Ethical Considerations: Intentions contribute to ethical judgments about the rightness or wrongness of actions, regardless of outcomes.
  - Trust and Authenticity: Intentions influence perceptions of sincerity, trustworthiness, and authenticity in relationships and interactions.

3. Clarity and Communication:
  - Effective Communication: Clearly communicating intentions helps align actions with desired outcomes and prevents misunderstandings.
  - Consistency: Aligning actions consistently with stated intentions builds credibility and reinforces trust in personal and professional relationships.

How Actions Reflect True Intentions

The Wisdom of Discernment

Navigating Life's Good and Bad

Actions serve as tangible manifestations of intentions, providing insights into individuals' beliefs, values, and character. Evaluating actions helps discern alignment between stated intentions and actual behavior.

1. Consistency in Behavior:
   - Pattern of Behavior: Consistent actions over time indicate sincerity and commitment to stated intentions.
   - Alignment with Values: Actions that align with personal values and ethical principles reflect genuine intentions and integrity.

2. Impact on Others:
   - Observable Effects: Assessing the impact of actions on others reveals underlying intentions and motivations.
   - Empathy and Consideration: Actions that demonstrate empathy, consideration, and respect for others' well-being reflect genuine care and positive intentions.

3. Accountability and Responsibility:
   - Ownership of Actions: Taking responsibility for actions, regardless of outcomes, demonstrates integrity and accountability for intentions.
   - Adaptability: Adjusting actions in response to feedback and changing circumstances reflects adaptive intentions and willingness to learn and grow.

4. Contextual Understanding:
   - Situational Factors: Recognizing how situational factors influence actions provides context for understanding intentions and decision-making processes.
   - Adaptability: Adjusting actions in response to feedback and changing circumstances reflects adaptive intentions and willingness to learn and grow.

By evaluating both actions and intentions, individuals can make informed judgments, build trust in relationships, and align their behavior with their values and goals. This chapter explores the dynamics between actions and intentions, offering insights into assessing authenticity and ethical considerations in personal and professional interactions.

The Wisdom of Discernment
Navigating Life's Good and Bad

Chapter 12: Trust and Betrayal

Building Trust

Trust is the foundation of healthy relationships, essential for collaboration, intimacy, and effective communication. Building and maintaining trust involves consistent actions, transparency, and reliability.

1. Components of Trust:
  - Reliability: Consistently fulfilling commitments and obligations.
  - Honesty: Communicating truthfully and transparently.
  - Integrity: Acting in alignment with ethical principles and values.
  - Empathy: Demonstrating understanding and consideration for others' perspectives and feelings.

2. Strategies for Building Trust:
  - Consistency: Aligning actions with words to build credibility and reliability.
  - Open Communication: Encouraging honest and transparent communication to foster mutual understanding and clarity.
  - Respect Boundaries: Respecting personal boundaries and demonstrating empathy and respect for others' perspectives.
  - Accountability: Taking responsibility for mistakes and demonstrating a commitment to learning and growth.

Recognizing and Handling Betrayal

Betrayal involves the violation of trust, causing emotional pain, disillusionment, and fractured relationships. Recognizing signs of betrayal and navigating its aftermath requires resilience, introspection, and effective coping strategies.

1. Types of Betrayal:
  - Deception: Deliberate dishonesty or concealment of information.

- Disloyalty: Breach of loyalty or commitment to a relationship or organization.
- Broken Promises: Failure to fulfill commitments or obligations.

2. Signs of Betrayal:
  - Inconsistencies: Discrepancies between words and actions.
  - Secrecy: Withholding information or engaging in secretive behaviors.
  - Emotional Distance: Withdrawal or avoidance in interpersonal interactions.

3. Navigating Betrayal:
  - Processing Emotions: Acknowledging and validating feelings of hurt, anger, or betrayal.
  - Seeking Support: Connecting with trusted individuals or professionals for emotional support and guidance.
  - Setting Boundaries: Establishing clear boundaries to protect oneself from further harm or manipulation.
  - Forgiveness and Healing: Considering forgiveness as a personal choice to promote emotional healing and closure.

4. Rebuilding Trust:
  - Transparency and Accountability: Demonstrating genuine remorse, transparency, and accountability for actions.
  - Consistent Effort: Committing to rebuilding trust through consistent actions and behaviors over time.
  - Communication and Understanding: Engaging in open dialogue to address concerns, clarify misunderstandings, and rebuild mutual understanding.

By exploring the dynamics of trust and betrayal, individuals can cultivate healthier relationships, navigate challenges with resilience, and make informed decisions about rebuilding trust or moving forward from betrayal. This chapter provides insights and practical strategies for fostering trust and resilience in personal and professional contexts.

Chapter 13: Influence of Social Media

The Good and Bad of Online Interactions

The Wisdom of Discernment
Navigating Life's Good and Bad

Social media platforms have revolutionized communication, connectivity, and information sharing, but they also pose challenges and risks that impact individuals' well-being and relationships.

1. Benefits of Social Media:
   - Global Connectivity: Facilitates instant communication and interaction with individuals worldwide.
   - Information Access: Provides access to a vast array of information, news, and resources.
   - Community Building: Fosters communities of shared interests, support networks, and collective action.
   - Promotion and Networking: Enables individuals and businesses to promote products, services, and professional connections.

2. Challenges and Risks:
   - Digital Footprint: Permanent record of online activities that can impact reputation and privacy.
   - Cyberbullying and Harassment: Exposure to negative interactions, harassment, or bullying.
   - Misinformation: Spread of false information and echo chambers that reinforce biases.
   - Comparison and Self-Esteem: Potential for social comparison, unrealistic standards, and negative effects on self-esteem.

Managing Digital Relationships

Navigating digital relationships requires awareness, boundaries, and mindful engagement to foster meaningful connections while mitigating potential risks and challenges.

1. Establishing Boundaries:
   - Privacy Settings: Adjusting privacy settings to control visibility and protect personal information.
   - Time Management: Setting limits on screen time and balancing online interactions with offline activities.

- Authenticity: Maintaining authenticity in online interactions and avoiding over-reliance on curated personas.

2. Building Healthy Habits:

- Mindful Consumption: Being selective about the content consumed and its impact on emotions and well-being.

- Positive Engagement: Contributing positively to online communities, promoting constructive dialogue, and supporting others.

- Critical Thinking: Questioning information sources, verifying facts, and avoiding the spread of misinformation.

3. Managing Conflict and Challenges:

- Conflict Resolution: Handling disagreements or misunderstandings diplomatically and respectfully.

- Seeking Support: Reaching out to trusted individuals or resources for guidance and emotional support during challenging online interactions.

- Self-Care: Prioritizing self-care practices to manage stress, anxiety, or emotional reactions triggered by online interactions.

4. Cultivating Meaningful Connections:

- Quality Over Quantity: Focusing on building genuine connections based on shared interests, values, and mutual respect.

- Offline Engagement: Balancing online interactions with face-to-face connections and meaningful offline activities.

- Empathy and Understanding: Practicing empathy and understanding in digital interactions to foster positive relationships and resolve conflicts effectively.

By understanding the dual nature of social media and adopting mindful practices for managing digital relationships, individuals can harness its benefits while mitigating risks, promoting well-being, and nurturing meaningful connections in both online and offline realms. This chapter offers practical insights and strategies for navigating the influence of social media in personal and professional contexts.

The Wisdom of Discernment
Navigating Life's Good and Bad

Chapter 14: Personal Values and Principles

Defining Your Core Values

Personal values are fundamental beliefs and principles that guide behavior, decisions, and interactions. Identifying and understanding your core values is essential for living authentically and aligning actions with your beliefs.

1. Identifying Core Values:
   - Reflection: Engage in self-reflection to identify beliefs, qualities, and principles that are most important to you.
   - Prioritization: Rank values based on their significance in shaping your priorities and decision-making.
   - Consistency: Assess whether values remain consistent across different aspects of life and align with long-term goals.

2. Types of Core Values:
   - Ethical Values: Integrity, honesty, fairness, and accountability in actions and relationships.
   - Personal Growth: Continuous learning, self-improvement, and pursuing challenges.
   - Family and Relationships: Prioritizing relationships, support, and emotional connections.
   - Community and Contribution: Making a positive impact, social responsibility, and empathy towards others.

Using Values as a Guide

Integrating core values into daily life provides a framework for making decisions, setting goals, and navigating challenges with clarity and purpose.

1. Decision-Making Framework:
   - Alignment: Evaluate decisions based on how well they align with your core values and principles.
   - Consistency: Ensure actions and choices reflect your values consistently over time.

- Prioritization: Use values to prioritize goals and commitments that are meaningful and fulfilling.

2. Setting Boundaries and Goals:
  - Boundary Setting: Establish boundaries that uphold your values and protect personal well-being in relationships and work environments.
  - Goal Setting: Set goals that are aligned with your values to enhance motivation, fulfillment, and a sense of purpose.

3. Navigating Challenges:
  - Resilience: Draw on values to maintain resilience during setbacks, adversity, or conflicts.
  - Ethical Dilemmas: Use values as a moral compass to guide ethical decision-making and actions.

4. Communicating Values:
  - Authenticity: Communicate values through actions and behaviors, fostering trust and respect in relationships.
  - Inspiration: Inspire others by exemplifying values in leadership, mentorship, and community involvement.

By defining your core values and integrating them into decision-making processes and daily actions, you can cultivate authenticity, purpose, and fulfillment in personal and professional endeavors. This chapter provides practical guidance for identifying, prioritizing, and applying personal values as a guiding force in shaping a meaningful and values-driven life.

Chapter 15: Ethical Decision Making

Frameworks for Making Ethical Choices

Ethical decision making involves considering moral principles, values, and consequences to determine the right course of action. Adopting ethical frameworks provides structure and guidance in navigating complex ethical dilemmas.

The Wisdom of Discernment

Navigating Life's Good and Bad

1. Utilitarianism:
 - Principle: Maximizing overall happiness or utility for the greatest number of people.
  - Application: Evaluate actions based on their outcomes and consequences, aiming to produce the greatest good and minimize harm.

2. Deontology:
 - Principle: Adherence to moral rules, duties, or principles, regardless of outcomes.
 - Application: Determine the rightness or wrongness of actions based on moral obligations, rights, and principles, such as honesty, fairness, or respect for autonomy.

3. Virtue Ethics:
 - Principle: Emphasis on the development of virtuous character traits and moral excellence.
  - Application: Consider how actions contribute to the cultivation of virtues, such as honesty, compassion, integrity, and courage.

4. Ethical Relativism:
  - Principle: Recognition of cultural, situational, or personal context in determining ethical standards.
  - Application: Evaluate actions based on the norms, values, and beliefs prevalent in specific contexts, acknowledging diverse perspectives on ethics.

Real-life Applications

Applying ethical decision-making frameworks to real-life scenarios promotes integrity, fairness, and responsible behavior in personal and professional contexts.

1. Professional Ethics:
  - Business Ethics: Addressing dilemmas related to corporate governance, environmental sustainability, and stakeholder interests.
  - Medical Ethics: Balancing patient autonomy, beneficence, and justice in healthcare decisions.
  - Legal Ethics: Upholding integrity, confidentiality, and fairness in legal practice and advocacy.

2. Personal Ethics:

   - Relationships: Navigating dilemmas involving honesty, loyalty, and respect in interpersonal interactions.

   - Personal Finance: Making decisions about investments, expenditures, and financial responsibilities with integrity and accountability.

   - Social Responsibility: Engaging in charitable activities, environmental stewardship, and community service aligned with ethical values.

3. Leadership and Decision Making:

   - Integrity and Transparency: Demonstrating ethical leadership by setting a positive example and fostering a culture of trust and accountability.

   - Conflict Resolution: Resolving conflicts and making decisions that balance ethical considerations and organizational objectives.

4. Ethical Reflection and Growth:

   - Continuous Learning: Reflecting on past decisions, seeking feedback, and learning from ethical challenges to improve decision-making skills.

   - Adaptability: Adapting ethical frameworks to evolving circumstances and emerging ethical dilemmas in a globalized and interconnected world.

By applying ethical decision-making frameworks and principles to diverse situations, individuals can promote ethical awareness, integrity, and responsible behavior in personal and professional life. This chapter offers practical guidance and examples for navigating ethical dilemmas and making principled decisions aligned with moral values and societal expectations.

Chapter 16: The Role of Honesty

Recognizing Honest and Dishonest Behaviors

The Wisdom of Discernment
Navigating Life's Good and Bad

Honesty is a fundamental virtue that fosters trust, integrity, and authenticity in personal and professional relationships. Recognizing honest and dishonest behaviors involves understanding the principles of truthfulness and transparency.

1. Characteristics of Honest Behaviors:
   - Truthfulness: Consistently communicating facts, opinions, and intentions accurately and sincerely.
   - Transparency: Openly sharing information, motivations, and actions without deception or concealment.
   - Accountability: Taking responsibility for one's actions, admitting mistakes, and seeking to rectify errors.

2. Indicators of Dishonest Behaviors:
   - Deception: Intentionally misleading others through lies, omissions, or half-truths to gain advantage or avoid consequences.
   - Manipulation: Using deceitful tactics or psychological strategies to influence or control others' perceptions or actions.
   - Betrayal of Trust: Violating commitments, agreements, or promises without genuine justification or consideration for others' well-being.

Encouraging Honesty in Yourself and Others

Promoting a culture of honesty involves cultivating personal integrity, fostering open communication, and setting expectations for ethical behavior in individuals and communities.

1. Personal Integrity:
   - Self-Awareness: Reflecting on personal values, beliefs, and motivations to align actions with principles of honesty and integrity.
   - Consistency: Demonstrating honesty consistently in words, actions, and decisions to build credibility and trustworthiness.

2. Creating a Trusting Environment:

- Open Communication: Encouraging transparent dialogue and active listening to facilitate honest exchanges of information and feedback.

- Setting Expectations: Establishing clear guidelines, policies, and ethical standards that emphasize the importance of honesty and integrity.

3. Promoting Ethical Leadership:

- Leading by Example: Modeling honest behavior and ethical decision-making as a leader or role model in personal and professional settings.

- Accountability and Consequences: Holding oneself and others accountable for dishonest actions while providing opportunities for learning and growth.

4. Building Trusting Relationships:

- Building Rapport: Establishing mutual respect, empathy, and understanding in relationships to create a foundation of trust.

- Conflict Resolution: Addressing misunderstandings or conflicts with honesty, empathy, and a commitment to finding mutually agreeable solutions.

By recognizing the importance of honesty, identifying honest and dishonest behaviors, and fostering a culture of integrity and transparency, individuals can cultivate meaningful relationships, promote ethical conduct, and contribute to a more trustworthy and respectful society. This chapter provides practical insights and strategies for embracing honesty as a cornerstone of personal and collective well-being.

Chapter 17: Respect and Disrespect

Identifying Respectful and Disrespectful Actions

Respect is a fundamental value that promotes dignity, fairness, and consideration for others. Recognizing respectful and disrespectful actions involves understanding behaviors that honor or undermine the rights and feelings of individuals.

1. Characteristics of Respectful Actions:

- Acknowledgment: Recognizing and valuing the perspectives, feelings, and contributions of others.
- Empathy: Demonstrating understanding and compassion towards others' experiences, beliefs, and boundaries.
- Fairness: Treating others impartially and equitably, respecting their rights and autonomy.

2. Indicators of Disrespectful Actions:
- Disregard: Ignoring or dismissing the opinions, feelings, or boundaries of others without consideration.
- Insensitivity: Behaving in a manner that causes harm, offense, or discomfort to others' dignity or well-being.
- Discrimination: Engaging in prejudiced or biased behaviors based on characteristics such as race, gender, religion, or socioeconomic status.

Cultivating a Culture of Respect

Promoting a culture of respect involves fostering mutual understanding, empathy, and inclusivity in personal, professional, and community settings.

1. Communication and Listening:
- Active Listening: Engaging attentively and empathetically to understand and validate others' perspectives and emotions.
- Constructive Feedback: Providing feedback respectfully and constructively, focusing on behaviors and outcomes rather than personal attributes.

2. Valuing Diversity and Inclusion:
- Celebrating Differences: Embracing diversity of backgrounds, perspectives, and experiences as enriching contributions to collective understanding and growth.
- Equity and Justice: Advocating for fairness, equality, and social justice to combat discrimination and promote inclusive environments.

3. Setting Boundaries and Consent:

- Respecting Boundaries: Honoring personal space, privacy, and autonomy by seeking consent and permission in interactions.

- Conflict Resolution: Resolving conflicts peacefully and respectfully, prioritizing reconciliation and understanding over escalation.

4. Leadership and Role Modeling:

- Leading by Example: Demonstrating respect through actions, decisions, and interactions as a leader or influential figure in organizations and communities.

- Promoting Accountability: Holding oneself and others accountable for upholding respectful behaviors and addressing instances of disrespect promptly and effectively.

By identifying respectful and disrespectful actions, fostering a culture of mutual respect, and embracing diversity and inclusivity, individuals contribute to creating supportive, harmonious, and thriving environments where everyone feels valued and heard. This chapter provides practical strategies and insights for promoting respect as a cornerstone of ethical conduct and positive relationships in various contexts of life.

Chapter 18: Healthy vs. Toxic Relationships

Characteristics of Healthy Relationships

Healthy relationships are built on mutual respect, trust, communication, and support. Recognizing the characteristics of healthy relationships helps individuals foster positive connections and emotional well-being.

1. Communication and Respect:

- Open Communication: Engaging in honest, transparent dialogue that fosters understanding and emotional intimacy.

- Respectful Interactions: Valuing each other's opinions, boundaries, and autonomy while demonstrating empathy and consideration.

2. Trust and Support:

- Reliability: Consistently being there for each other and honoring commitments.

- Emotional Support: Providing encouragement, empathy, and validation during challenging times.

3. Equality and Independence:
  - Balance: Maintaining a balance of power and decision-making in the relationship.
  - Individuality: Respecting each other's independence, interests, and personal growth.

4. Conflict Resolution:
  - Constructive Conflict: Addressing disagreements calmly and respectfully, seeking mutually acceptable resolutions.
  - Compromise: Willingness to negotiate and find solutions that meet both partners' needs.

Identifying and Escaping Toxic Relationships

Toxic relationships are characterized by unhealthy behaviors, manipulation, and emotional or psychological harm. Recognizing signs of toxicity and taking steps to remove oneself from such relationships are crucial for emotional well-being and personal growth.

1. Signs of Toxic Relationships:
  - Control and Manipulation: Exerting control over decisions, behaviors, or interactions through manipulation or coercion.
  - Disrespect and Demeaning Behavior: Belittling, criticizing, or undermining each other's self-esteem and worth.
  - Lack of Trust and Support: Consistently breaking promises, betraying trust, or failing to provide emotional support.

2. Emotional and Psychological Impact:
  - Stress and Anxiety: Feeling constantly drained, anxious, or insecure due to the relationship dynamics.
  - Isolation: Being isolated from friends, family, or support networks as a result of the relationship.

3. Steps to Escaping Toxic Relationships:

- Self-Assessment: Reflecting on the relationship dynamics and recognizing patterns of toxicity.
- Setting Boundaries: Establishing clear boundaries and limits to protect emotional well-being and personal boundaries.
- Seeking Support: Reaching out to trusted friends, family members, or professionals for guidance and emotional support.
- Exiting Safely: Planning a safe exit strategy if necessary, considering legal, financial, and logistical aspects.

4. Recovery and Healing:
- Self-Care: Prioritizing self-care practices to heal emotionally and regain confidence and self-worth.
- Professional Help: Seeking counseling or therapy to process emotions, heal from trauma, and rebuild self-esteem.

By understanding the characteristics of healthy relationships and recognizing signs of toxicity, individuals can cultivate supportive, respectful connections that promote personal growth, happiness, and emotional well-being. This chapter provides practical guidance for navigating relationship dynamics and making informed decisions about fostering healthy relationships and exiting toxic ones.

Chapter 19: Conflict Resolution

Handling Disagreements Constructively

Conflict resolution is the process of addressing disagreements or disputes in a way that promotes understanding, cooperation, and mutual respect. Effective conflict resolution skills are essential for maintaining healthy relationships and fostering positive outcomes.

1. Active Listening and Empathy:
- Listen Actively: Paying attention to the other person's perspective without interrupting, demonstrating empathy and understanding.

The Wisdom of Discernment
Navigating Life's Good and Bad

- Validate Feelings: Acknowledging the emotions and concerns expressed by the other person to establish rapport and trust.

2. Clarifying Issues and Needs:
- Define the Problem: Clearly articulating the specific issue or concern at hand to avoid misunderstandings.
- Identify Needs: Discussing each party's underlying needs, interests, and priorities to find common ground.

3. Seeking Win-Win Solutions:
- Brainstorming: Generating multiple possible solutions or compromises that address the interests of both parties.
- Negotiation: Collaboratively discussing and adjusting proposals to reach a mutually acceptable agreement.

4. Maintaining Respect and Communication:
- Respectful Communication: Using assertive, non-confrontational language and tone to express thoughts and feelings.
- Avoid Blame: Focusing on the issue at hand rather than assigning blame or criticism.

When to Walk Away

Sometimes, despite efforts to resolve conflict constructively, it may become necessary to disengage from a situation that is unhealthy, unproductive, or harmful to one's well-being.

1. Signs to Consider Walking Away:
- Repeated Patterns: Persistent conflicts that do not lead to resolution or improvement over time.
- Emotional or Physical Safety: Situations where continued engagement poses risks to emotional or physical well-being.
- Lack of Respect: Disrespectful behavior, manipulation, or abuse that undermines personal boundaries and dignity.

2. Assessing Impact and Consequences:

  - Personal Boundaries: Recognizing when the conflict violates personal values, boundaries, or principles.

  - Long-term Well-being: Considering the emotional, psychological, and relational impact of prolonged conflict on oneself and others involved.

3. Seeking Support and Guidance:

   - Consulting Trusted Advisors: Seeking advice from friends, family members, or professionals who can provide objective perspectives and guidance.

  - Professional Help: Engaging a mediator, counselor, or therapist to facilitate constructive dialogue or support decision-making.

4. Self-Care and Healing:

  - Prioritizing Self-Care: Taking time to process emotions, practice self-care, and nurture emotional resilience.

  - Reflecting and Learning: Reflecting on the conflict experience to learn from it, identify personal growth opportunities, and set boundaries for future interactions.

By developing skills in constructive conflict resolution and knowing when to disengage from unhealthy situations, individuals can navigate disagreements effectively, preserve relationships, and prioritize their well-being and personal growth. This chapter provides practical strategies for managing conflicts and making informed decisions about resolving disputes or walking away when necessary.

Chapter 20: Self-awareness and Reflection

The Importance of Knowing Yourself

Self-awareness is the ability to introspectively understand one's own thoughts, emotions, motivations, and behaviors. It plays a crucial role in personal growth, decision-making, and building fulfilling relationships.

1. Clarity and Direction:

The Wisdom of Discernment
Navigating Life's Good and Bad

- Identifying Strengths and Weaknesses: Recognizing your unique qualities, skills, and areas for improvement.
- Setting Personal Goals: Aligning goals and aspirations with your values, interests, and long-term vision.

2. Emotional Intelligence:
- Managing Emotions: Understanding and regulating your emotions effectively, which enhances resilience and interpersonal relationships.
- Empathy: Developing empathy towards others' perspectives and feelings, fostering deeper connections and communication.

3. Authenticity and Integrity:
- Consistency: Aligning actions with values and beliefs, promoting authenticity in interactions and decision-making.
- Building Trust: Demonstrating reliability and accountability, which strengthens trust in personal and professional relationships.

4. Personal Development:
- Continuous Learning: Embracing opportunities for growth, self-improvement, and lifelong learning.
- Adaptability: Adapting to changes and challenges with resilience and a growth mindset.

Techniques for Self-reflection

Self-reflection involves deliberate introspection and assessment of thoughts, feelings, and experiences to gain insight and promote personal development.

1. Journaling:
- Writing Prompts: Using prompts to explore thoughts, emotions, challenges, and achievements.
- Gratitude Journal: Reflecting on moments of gratitude and positive experiences to cultivate optimism and mindfulness.

2. Mindfulness Practices:

   - Meditation: Practicing mindfulness meditation to enhance self-awareness, focus, and emotional regulation.

   - Breath Awareness: Using focused breathing exercises to center yourself and observe thoughts and sensations without judgment.

3. Feedback and Self-assessment:

   - Seeking Feedback: Requesting input from trusted individuals, mentors, or peers to gain external perspectives and insights.

   - Self-assessment Tools: Utilizing personality assessments, strengths assessments, or career aptitude tests to gain deeper self-understanding.

4. Setting Aside Quiet Time:

   - Solitude: Creating moments of solitude and quiet to reflect, recharge, and connect with inner thoughts and feelings.

   - Nature Walks: Taking walks or spending time in nature to promote relaxation, creativity, and introspection.

5. Goal Setting and Review:

   - SMART Goals: Setting Specific, Measurable, Achievable, Relevant, and Time-bound goals, and regularly reviewing progress and adjustments.

   - Reflection on Achievements: Celebrating accomplishments and milestones, reflecting on lessons learned, and planning next steps for growth.

By cultivating self-awareness through introspection and reflection, individuals enhance their emotional intelligence, authenticity, and personal growth. This chapter offers practical techniques and insights to support ongoing self-discovery and development in various aspects of life.

Chapter 21: Setting Boundaries

Why Boundaries are Crucial

The Wisdom of Discernment

Navigating Life's Good and Bad

Boundaries are essential guidelines that define personal limits, expectations, and acceptable behavior in relationships and interactions. They are crucial for maintaining emotional well-being, self-respect, and healthy dynamics.

1. Self-Preservation and Well-being:
  - Protecting Personal Space: Establishing limits on personal time, energy, and resources to prevent burnout and maintain balance.
  - Emotional Protection: Safeguarding emotional health by setting boundaries that prevent manipulation, emotional abuse, or excessive demands.

2. Respect and Empowerment:
  - Respecting Autonomy: Asserting individual needs, preferences, and values, promoting mutual respect and understanding.
  - Empowering Relationships: Fostering relationships built on trust, transparency, and mutual support through clear communication of boundaries.

3. Clarifying Expectations:
  - Defining Roles and Responsibilities: Clarifying roles and expectations in professional and personal relationships to avoid misunderstandings and conflict.
  - Promoting Accountability: Holding oneself and others accountable for respecting agreed-upon boundaries and maintaining healthy interactions.

How to Set and Maintain Boundaries

Setting and maintaining boundaries involves self-awareness, assertiveness, and effective communication to establish and enforce personal limits respectfully.

1. Identify Your Limits:
  - Self-assessment: Reflecting on personal values, needs, and comfort levels to determine where boundaries are needed.
  - Recognize Triggers: Identifying situations or behaviors that signal the need for boundary setting to protect emotional well-being.

2. Communicate Clearly and Assertively:

  - Direct Communication: Clearly articulating boundaries, expectations, and consequences in a straightforward manner.

  - Use "I" Statements: Expressing feelings, needs, and boundaries using assertive language without blaming or criticizing others.

3. Enforce Boundaries Consistently:

  - Follow Through: Maintaining consistency in upholding boundaries and addressing violations promptly and assertively.

  - Self-care: Prioritizing self-care practices to recharge and reinforce personal boundaries, demonstrating commitment to self-respect and well-being.

4. Seek Support and Feedback:

  - Consult Trusted Individuals: Seeking guidance from supportive friends, family members, or mentors who respect boundaries and provide constructive feedback.

  - Professional Help: Consulting therapists or counselors for guidance in boundary setting and maintaining healthy relationships, particularly in challenging or complex situations.

5. Evaluate and Adjust as Needed:

  - Reflection: Periodically reflecting on boundary effectiveness, reassessing needs, and adjusting boundaries as personal circumstances or relationships evolve.

  - Flexibility: Remaining open to negotiation and compromise while maintaining core boundaries that safeguard well-being and integrity.

By prioritizing self-awareness, assertiveness, and clear communication, individuals can establish and maintain boundaries that promote self-respect, healthy relationships, and emotional well-being. This chapter offers practical strategies and insights for navigating the complexities of boundary setting in various aspects of life.

Chapter 22: The Power of Forgiveness

Understanding Forgiveness

The Wisdom of Discernment
Navigating Life's Good and Bad

Forgiveness is a transformative process that involves letting go of resentment, anger, or bitterness towards someone who has caused harm or offense. It promotes healing, reconciliation, and emotional well-being for both the forgiver and the forgiven.

1. Release and Healing:
   - Letting Go of Resentment: Releasing negative emotions and freeing oneself from the burden of anger or hurt.
   - Emotional Liberation: Achieving emotional freedom and peace by forgiving past grievances or injustices.

2. Empathy and Understanding:
   - Compassion: Cultivating empathy towards the person who caused harm, acknowledging their humanity and potential for growth.
   - Perspective-taking: Considering the circumstances or motivations behind the offense to gain a broader understanding of the situation.

3. Personal Growth and Resilience:
   - Self-reflection: Reflecting on personal values, beliefs, and experiences to gain insight and perspective on forgiveness.
   - Building Resilience: Strengthening emotional resilience and coping mechanisms through forgiveness, which enhances psychological well-being.

How to Forgive Without Forgetting

Forgiving without forgetting involves acknowledging past experiences while choosing to release negative emotions and move forward with wisdom and self-protection.

1. Acknowledge and Validate Feelings:
   - Honor Emotions: Recognizing and processing feelings of hurt, betrayal, or anger as valid reactions to the offense.
   - Self-compassion: Practicing self-compassion and self-care to nurture emotional well-being during the forgiveness process.

2. Set Boundaries and Protect Yourself:

 - Healthy Boundaries: Establishing clear boundaries to protect oneself from further harm or recurrence of the offense.

 - Assertiveness: Asserting personal needs and expectations in relationships while promoting mutual respect and understanding.

3. Seeking Closure and Resolution:

 - Communication: Engaging in honest and constructive dialogue with the person involved, if appropriate, to seek closure and understanding.

 - Conflict Resolution: Resolving misunderstandings or conflicts through empathetic listening, mutual respect, and collaborative problem-solving.

4. Learning and Growth:

 - Extracting Lessons: Identifying lessons learned from the experience to promote personal growth, resilience, and wisdom.

 - Forgiving Yourself: Extending forgiveness to oneself for any perceived shortcomings or mistakes related to the situation.

5. Embracing Forgiveness as a Process:

 - Time and Patience: Allowing time for emotional healing and forgiveness to unfold gradually, respecting one's own pace and readiness.

 - Cultivating Forgiveness: Practicing forgiveness as a conscious choice and ongoing process, fostering empathy, compassion, and inner peace.

By understanding the transformative power of forgiveness, individuals can heal emotional wounds, promote reconciliation, and cultivate greater compassion and resilience in personal and interpersonal relationships. This chapter offers practical insights and strategies for embracing forgiveness as a path to emotional freedom and growth.

Chapter 23: Kindness and Compassion

The Impact of Kindness

The Wisdom of Discernment
Navigating Life's Good and Bad

Kindness is a powerful virtue that involves showing empathy, generosity, and goodwill towards others. It has profound positive effects on individuals, relationships, and communities, fostering a culture of empathy and connection.

1. Promoting Well-being:

  - Emotional Benefits: Boosting mood, reducing stress, and promoting a sense of happiness and fulfillment for both the giver and recipient.

  - Social Bonds: Strengthening interpersonal relationships and building trust, reciprocity, and cooperation within communities.

2. Cultivating Positivity:

  - Positive Ripple Effect: Inspiring others to act with kindness, creating a ripple effect of positivity and compassion in society.

  - Creating Meaningful Connections: Establishing meaningful connections and fostering a sense of belonging and support.

3. Building Resilience:

  - Emotional Resilience: Enhancing emotional resilience by fostering a supportive environment and mutual care.

  - Overcoming Adversity: Helping individuals and communities cope with challenges and adversity through acts of kindness and compassion.

Practicing Compassion in Daily Life

Compassion involves empathizing with others' suffering or challenges and taking action to alleviate their pain or support their well-being. Integrating compassion into daily life promotes empathy, understanding, and a sense of shared humanity.

1. Empathetic Listening:

  - Active Listening: Engaging attentively and empathetically to understand others' perspectives, emotions, and needs.

  - Validation: Acknowledging and validating others' feelings and experiences to promote emotional healing and connection.

2. Acts of Kindness:

- Random Acts of Kindness: Performing spontaneous acts of generosity, such as offering assistance, compliments, or acts of service.

- Intentional Acts: Deliberately choosing kindness in interactions and relationships, fostering a culture of compassion and respect.

3. Supporting Others:

- Empowerment: Encouraging and supporting others' growth, well-being, and personal development through encouragement and practical assistance.

- Social Justice: Advocating for fairness, equality, and social justice to address systemic issues and promote a more compassionate society.

4. Self-compassion:

- Self-care: Practicing self-compassion and self-care to nurture emotional well-being, resilience, and a positive mindset.

- Balancing Needs: Balancing personal needs with acts of compassion towards others, fostering a healthy sense of self-worth and fulfillment.

5. Mindful Living:

- Mindfulness Practices: Cultivating mindfulness to enhance awareness of one's thoughts, feelings, and actions, promoting intentional and compassionate living.

- Reflection and Gratitude: Reflecting on acts of kindness and expressing gratitude for opportunities to make a positive impact on others' lives.

By embracing kindness and compassion in daily life, individuals contribute to creating a more empathetic, supportive, and interconnected community. This chapter provides practical strategies and insights for integrating kindness and compassion into personal values, interactions, and societal contributions.

Chapter 24: Manipulation Tactics

Recognizing Manipulative Behaviors

The Wisdom of Discernment

Navigating Life's Good and Bad

Manipulation involves using deceptive or exploitative tactics to influence or control others' thoughts, feelings, or actions for personal gain or advantage. Recognizing manipulative behaviors is essential for maintaining autonomy, boundaries, and healthy relationships.

1. Common Manipulative Tactics:

  - Gaslighting: Manipulating someone into questioning their own perceptions, memories, or sanity.

  - Guilt Tripping: Using guilt or obligation to manipulate others into compliance or specific behaviors.

  - Love Bombing: Overwhelming someone with excessive attention, affection, or praise to gain control or influence.

  - Silent Treatment: Using silence or withdrawal as a form of emotional manipulation or punishment.

  - Selective Truth-Telling: Distorting or selectively presenting information to influence perceptions or decisions.

  - Playing the Victim: portraying oneself as a victim to garner sympathy, manipulate emotions, or avoid accountability.

2. Psychological and Emotional Impact:

  - Undermining Confidence: Degrading self-confidence, self-esteem, or self-worth to maintain control or power.

  - Creating Dependency: Fostering dependency or reliance on the manipulator for validation, approval, or decision-making.

  - Isolation: Manipulating social relationships or dynamics to isolate individuals from support networks or alternative perspectives.

Protecting Yourself from Manipulation

Protecting oneself from manipulation involves developing awareness, setting boundaries, and assertively responding to manipulative tactics to safeguard emotional well-being and autonomy.

1. Cultivate Self-awareness:

  - Trust Your Instincts: Pay attention to gut feelings or intuition that signal discomfort or suspicion of manipulative behavior.

  - Reflect on Patterns: Recognize recurring patterns of manipulation or coercion in relationships or interactions.

2. Set and Enforce Boundaries:

  - Clear Communication: Assertively communicate personal boundaries, values, and expectations to prevent manipulation.

  - Consistency: Maintain consistency in upholding boundaries and responding assertively to manipulative tactics.

3. Practice Assertiveness:

  - Assertive Communication: Use clear, direct communication to express thoughts, feelings, and needs while respecting others' boundaries.

  - Refuse Manipulative Demands: Decline requests or demands that compromise personal values, priorities, or well-being.

4. Seek Support and Validation:

  - Consult Trusted Advisors: Seek guidance from friends, family members, or professionals who can provide objective perspectives and support.

  - Therapeutic Support: Consider therapy or counseling to process experiences of manipulation, rebuild self-confidence, and develop healthy coping strategies.

5. Educate Yourself:

  - Awareness of Tactics: Educate yourself about common manipulation tactics and psychological principles to recognize and resist manipulation effectively.

  - Critical Thinking: Practice critical thinking and evaluate information or requests based on factual evidence and objective reasoning.

By recognizing manipulative behaviors, setting boundaries, and practicing assertiveness and self-care, individuals can protect themselves from manipulation and maintain healthy, respectful relationships built on trust and mutual respect. This chapter provides practical strategies and insights for identifying and responding to manipulation effectively in various aspects of life.

Chapter 25: Support Systems

Building and Maintaining Support Networks

Support systems are essential networks of individuals, resources, and communities that provide emotional, practical, and social support during challenging times, fostering resilience and well-being.

1. Identifying Supportive Relationships:
 - Personal Connections: Cultivating relationships with friends, family members, or mentors who offer empathy, encouragement, and understanding.
 - Professional Networks: Engaging with colleagues, mentors, or peers in professional settings to exchange knowledge, advice, and support.

2. Types of Support:
 - Emotional Support: Receiving empathy, validation, and comfort during times of stress, grief, or uncertainty.
 - Practical Support: Obtaining tangible assistance, such as childcare, transportation, or financial assistance during crises or life transitions.
 - Informational Support: Accessing advice, guidance, or resources to make informed decisions or navigate challenges effectively.

3. Building Trust and Reciprocity:
 - Mutual Exchange: Establishing reciprocal relationships where support and assistance are offered and received mutually.
 - Open Communication: Maintaining open, honest communication to express needs, boundaries, and expectations within support networks.

The Role of Community

The Wisdom of Discernment
Navigating Life's Good and Bad

Communities play a crucial role in providing a sense of belonging, connection, and collective support, enhancing individual well-being and societal resilience.

1. Shared Identity and Belonging:
 - Cultural or Interest-Based Communities: Participating in communities that share common values, traditions, or interests to foster a sense of identity and belonging.
 - Local Communities: Engaging with neighbors, local organizations, or community groups to promote collaboration, social cohesion, and community resilience.

2. Social Support Networks:
 - Social Connections: Building social connections and networks within communities to access emotional support, social activities, and mutual assistance.
 - Volunteerism and Service: Contributing to community initiatives, volunteering, or participating in collective efforts to address shared challenges or promote social causes.

3. Crisis and Disaster Response:
 - Community Resilience: Mobilizing collective resources, support, and resilience in response to crises, disasters, or emergencies affecting the community.
 - Recovery and Rebuilding: Collaborating with community members and organizations to facilitate recovery, rebuild infrastructure, and support affected individuals or families.

4. Promoting Well-being and Social Equity:
 - Advocacy and Empowerment: Advocating for social justice, equity, and inclusivity within communities to address systemic barriers and promote well-being for all members.
 - Resource Sharing: Sharing resources, knowledge, and skills within communities to empower individuals, strengthen social connections, and promote collective prosperity.

By actively building and nurturing support networks and engaging with communities, individuals can cultivate resilience, well-being, and a sense of belonging. This chapter provides practical strategies and insights for creating and maintaining supportive relationships and harnessing the collective strength of communities for personal and collective growth.

Chapter 26: Financial Discernment

Making Wise Financial Decisions

Financial discernment involves making informed, thoughtful decisions regarding money management, investments, and financial planning to achieve long-term financial stability and goals.

1. Setting Financial Goals:
  - Short-term and Long-term Goals: Establishing specific, measurable goals such as savings targets, debt reduction, retirement planning, or investment milestones.
  - Aligning Goals with Values: Ensuring financial decisions align with personal values, priorities, and lifestyle aspirations.

2. Financial Literacy and Education:
  - Knowledge Acquisition: Educating oneself about financial concepts, tools, and strategies through courses, workshops, or reputable resources.
  - Understanding Risks and Returns: Evaluating investment risks, financial products, and potential returns to make informed decisions.

3. Budgeting and Financial Planning:
  - Creating a Budget: Developing a budget to track income, expenses, and savings goals, enabling proactive financial management and decision-making.
  - Emergency Fund: Establishing and maintaining an emergency fund to cover unexpected expenses or financial setbacks.

4. Seeking Professional Advice:
  - Financial Advisors: Consulting certified financial planners or advisors to receive personalized guidance, investment recommendations, and retirement planning strategies.
  - Legal and Tax Advice: Obtaining legal and tax advice to understand implications of financial decisions and optimize tax efficiency.

Avoiding Financial Pitfalls

The Wisdom of Discernment
Navigating Life's Good and Bad

Avoiding financial pitfalls involves identifying and mitigating risks, managing debt responsibly, and safeguarding financial well-being against common pitfalls.

1. Debt Management:
  - Debt Reduction Strategies: Implementing strategies to reduce high-interest debt, such as prioritizing payments, consolidating debt, or negotiating repayment terms.
  - Avoiding Debt Traps: Being cautious of predatory lending practices, high-interest loans, or excessive use of credit cards.

2. Building a Safety Net:
  - Insurance Coverage: Securing adequate insurance coverage for health, life, property, and disability to protect against financial losses due to unforeseen circumstances.
  - Planning for Retirement: Contributing to retirement savings accounts (e.g., 401(k), IRA) and exploring investment options for long-term financial security.

3. Evaluating Investments:
  - Diversification: Spreading investments across different asset classes (e.g., stocks, bonds, real estate) to reduce risk and maximize returns over time.
  - Research and Due Diligence: Conducting thorough research and due diligence before investing in stocks, mutual funds, or other financial instruments.

4. Consumer Awareness:
  - Avoiding Scams and Fraud: Recognizing common financial scams, fraudulent schemes, or misleading investment opportunities to protect personal finances.
  - Consumer Rights: Understanding consumer rights and protections related to financial products, services, and transactions.

By practicing financial discernment, individuals can make informed decisions, avoid potential pitfalls, and build a secure financial future aligned with their goals and values. This chapter offers practical strategies and insights for navigating financial challenges, maximizing opportunities, and achieving long-term financial well-being.

The Wisdom of Discernment
Navigating Life's Good and Bad

Chapter 27: Career and Purpose

Finding Fulfillment in Work

Finding fulfillment in work involves pursuing meaningful, satisfying, and rewarding professional experiences that align with personal interests, strengths, and aspirations.

1. Identifying Personal Passions and Strengths:
  - Self-assessment: Reflecting on personal interests, values, skills, and strengths to identify potential career paths or roles that align with individual preferences.
  - Exploring Options: Researching various industries, professions, or career fields to discover opportunities that spark passion and enthusiasm.

2. Seeking Meaningful Work:
  - Purpose-driven Careers: Pursuing careers or roles that contribute to a greater cause, societal impact, or personal fulfillment beyond financial rewards.
  - Job Satisfaction: Evaluating factors such as job autonomy, challenges, growth opportunities, and workplace culture to gauge potential job satisfaction.

3. Work-life Integration:
  - Balancing Priorities: Achieving a harmonious balance between professional responsibilities and personal interests, relationships, and well-being.
  - Flexibility and Wellness: Prioritizing work environments that promote work-life balance, flexibility, and employee well-being.

Aligning Career with Personal Values

Aligning career with personal values involves integrating core beliefs, principles, and ethical considerations into professional decision-making and workplace interactions.

1. Defining Core Values:
  - Identifying Values: Clarifying personal values related to integrity, ethics, social responsibility, diversity, sustainability, or innovation.

- Prioritizing Alignment: Evaluating potential employers, job roles, and organizational cultures to ensure alignment with personal values.

2. Ethical Decision-making:
  - Integrity and Accountability: Upholding ethical standards and principles in professional conduct, decision-making, and interactions with colleagues, clients, and stakeholders.
  - Navigating Challenges: Addressing ethical dilemmas or conflicts in the workplace with transparency, fairness, and respect for diverse perspectives.

3. Career Development and Growth:
  - Continuous Learning: Pursuing professional development opportunities, training, certifications, or advanced education to enhance skills and expertise in chosen career paths.
  - Goal Setting: Setting career goals and objectives that reflect personal values, aspirations, and desired outcomes for professional growth and achievement.

4. Impact and Legacy:
  - Contributing to Community: Engaging in volunteerism, mentorship, or community involvement to make a positive impact and leave a lasting legacy beyond professional achievements.
  - Sustainability and Long-term Impact: Considering environmental, social, and economic sustainability factors in career decisions to promote long-term societal benefits and well-being.

By prioritizing fulfillment, aligning career choices with personal values, and fostering a sense of purpose in work, individuals can cultivate meaningful professional experiences that contribute to personal growth, societal impact, and overall well-being. This chapter provides practical strategies and insights for navigating career decisions, finding fulfillment, and integrating personal values into professional pursuits.

Chapter 28: Health and Well-being

Identifying Positive Health Practices

The Wisdom of Discernment
Navigating Life's Good and Bad

Positive health practices encompass habits, behaviors, and attitudes that promote physical, mental, and emotional well-being, contributing to a balanced and healthy lifestyle.

1. Physical Health:
   - Nutrition: Adopting a balanced diet rich in nutrients, vitamins, and minerals to support overall health and energy levels.
   - Exercise: Incorporating regular physical activity, such as aerobic exercises, strength training, or flexibility exercises, to improve cardiovascular health, strength, and endurance.
   - Sleep: Prioritizing adequate sleep and establishing healthy sleep hygiene practices to promote restorative sleep and mental clarity.

2. Mental and Emotional Well-being:
   - Stress Management: Implementing stress-reduction techniques, such as mindfulness, meditation, deep breathing exercises, or yoga, to alleviate stress and promote relaxation.
   - Emotional Resilience: Building emotional resilience through self-care practices, positive coping mechanisms, and seeking support from loved ones or mental health professionals when needed.
   - Social Connections: Cultivating supportive relationships, social interactions, and meaningful connections with others to foster emotional well-being and reduce feelings of loneliness or isolation.

3. Preventive Health Care:
   - Regular Check-ups: Scheduling routine medical check-ups, screenings, and vaccinations to detect and prevent potential health issues early.
   - Health Monitoring: Monitoring health indicators, such as blood pressure, cholesterol levels, and weight, to maintain optimal health and wellness.
   - Health Education: Staying informed about health-related topics, conditions, and preventive measures through reliable sources and professional advice.

Avoiding Harmful Behaviors

Avoiding harmful behaviors involves recognizing and abstaining from practices that pose risks to physical, mental, or emotional health, promoting overall well-being and longevity.

The Wisdom of Discernment
Navigating Life's Good and Bad

1. Substance Abuse Prevention:

   - Alcohol and Drug Awareness: Understanding the risks associated with alcohol consumption, recreational drugs, or substance abuse and making informed decisions about moderation or abstinence.

   - Smoking Cessation: Seeking support and resources to quit smoking or avoid tobacco products to reduce the risk of tobacco-related diseases and improve respiratory health.

2. Healthy Relationships:

   - Boundaries and Respect: Establishing and maintaining boundaries in relationships to promote mutual respect, trust, and emotional well-being.

   - Conflict Resolution: Handling conflicts constructively and respectfully within relationships to nurture positive communication and understanding.

3. Safety and Injury Prevention:

   - Accident Prevention: Practicing safety measures and precautions in daily activities, such as wearing seat belts, using protective gear, and avoiding risky behaviors to prevent accidents or injuries.

   - Mental Health Support: Seeking professional help or counseling for mental health concerns, such as depression, anxiety, or trauma, to receive appropriate treatment and support.

4. Healthy Screen Time and Digital Wellness:

   - Balanced Technology Use: Managing screen time and digital device use to maintain a healthy balance between online activities, productivity, and offline interactions.

   - Cybersecurity Awareness: Practicing online safety measures, protecting personal information, and avoiding cyber threats to safeguard digital well-being and privacy.

By adopting positive health practices, avoiding harmful behaviors, and prioritizing well-being in physical, mental, and emotional aspects of life, individuals can enhance their quality of life, longevity, and overall happiness. This chapter offers practical strategies and insights for promoting health, preventing illness, and cultivating a holistic approach to well-being.

Chapter 29: Cultural and Societal Influences

Understanding Cultural Norms

Cultural norms encompass shared beliefs, values, traditions, and behaviors within a specific society or community, shaping individuals' identities, interactions, and perceptions of the world.

1. Cultural Diversity and Awareness:
   - Cultural Sensitivity: Demonstrating respect, openness, and acceptance towards diverse cultural perspectives, practices, and traditions.
   - Cross-cultural Communication: Developing effective communication skills to navigate cultural differences, promote mutual understanding, and avoid misunderstandings.

2. Impact on Identity and Belonging:
   - Cultural Identity: Exploring personal cultural identity, heritage, and traditions that influence individual perspectives, values, and sense of belonging.
   - Integration and Adaptation: Adapting to new cultural environments, norms, or societal expectations while preserving one's cultural identity and values.

3. Cultural Competence:
   - Understanding Cultural Context: Recognizing the influence of historical, social, and political factors on cultural norms and behaviors within different communities or societies.
   - Promoting Inclusivity: Advocating for inclusivity, diversity, and equity in cultural practices, policies, and societal institutions to foster a more inclusive and respectful society.

Balancing Societal Expectations and Personal Beliefs

Balancing societal expectations and personal beliefs involves navigating social pressures, norms, and cultural standards while staying true to individual values, principles, and ethical considerations.

1. Self-awareness and Authenticity:

The Wisdom of Discernment

Navigating Life's Good and Bad

- Self-reflection: Reflecting on personal values, beliefs, and principles to align actions, decisions, and behaviors with authentic self-expression.

- Integrity: Maintaining integrity by adhering to moral and ethical principles, even when facing societal pressures or conflicting expectations.

2. Navigating Cultural Norms:

- Critical Thinking: Evaluating societal norms, traditions, or expectations critically to discern their impact on personal choices, behaviors, and decision-making.

- Open Dialogue: Engaging in respectful dialogue and discussions with others to explore diverse perspectives, challenge assumptions, and promote mutual understanding.

3. Respecting Differences and Boundaries:

- Boundaries: Setting boundaries to protect personal values, beliefs, and autonomy while respecting the rights and perspectives of others within diverse cultural contexts.

- Conflict Resolution: Resolving conflicts or disagreements constructively by finding common ground, compromising, or negotiating mutually acceptable solutions.

4. Advocacy and Social Change:

- Social Justice: Advocating for social justice, equity, and inclusivity by challenging discriminatory practices, advocating for human rights, and promoting positive social change.

- Community Engagement: Participating in community initiatives, activism, or advocacy efforts to address societal issues and promote cultural understanding, respect, and unity.

By understanding cultural norms, embracing diversity, and navigating societal expectations while honoring personal beliefs and values, individuals can foster greater self-awareness, resilience, and harmony in personal and social interactions. This chapter provides practical strategies and insights for navigating cultural influences, promoting inclusivity, and fostering respectful engagement within diverse cultural and societal contexts.

Chapter 30: Personal Growth and Development

The Path to Self-improvement

The Wisdom of Discernment

Navigating Life's Good and Bad

Personal growth and development involve continuous learning, self-discovery, and intentional efforts to enhance skills, capabilities, and overall well-being.

1. Self-awareness and Reflection:
   - Self-assessment: Evaluating strengths, weaknesses, values, and aspirations to identify areas for personal growth and improvement.
   - Mindfulness: Cultivating mindfulness practices to enhance self-awareness, emotional regulation, and present-moment awareness.

2. Lifelong Learning:
   - Skill Development: Acquiring new skills, knowledge, and competencies through formal education, workshops, courses, or self-directed learning.
   - Professional Growth: Pursuing career advancement opportunities, certifications, or mentorship to achieve professional development goals.

3. Embracing Challenges and Growth Opportunities:
   - Comfort Zone Expansion: Stepping outside comfort zones to embrace challenges, take calculated risks, and foster personal resilience and adaptability.
   - Learning from Setbacks: Embracing failures or setbacks as opportunities for learning, growth, and personal development.

Setting and Achieving Goals

Setting and achieving goals provide structure, motivation, and direction for personal growth, enabling individuals to realize their aspirations and potential.

1. SMART Goals Framework:
   - Specific: Setting clear and specific goals that define what you want to achieve.
   - Measurable: Establishing criteria to track progress and measure success towards goal attainment.
   - Achievable: Setting realistic and attainable goals that align with personal capabilities, resources, and timelines.

- Relevant: Ensuring goals are relevant and meaningful to personal values, aspirations, and long-term objectives.
   - Time-bound: Establishing a timeframe or deadline to achieve goals, promoting accountability and motivation.

2. Action Planning and Implementation:
   - Breaking Down Goals: Breaking down larger goals into smaller, manageable tasks or milestones to facilitate progress and maintain momentum.
   - Prioritization and Focus: Prioritizing tasks, allocating resources effectively, and maintaining focus on achieving goals despite challenges or distractions.

3. Monitoring and Adaptation:
   - Progress Tracking: Monitoring progress towards goals, assessing achievements, and adjusting strategies or action plans as needed to stay on course.
   - Seeking Feedback: Seeking feedback from mentors, peers, or stakeholders to gain insights, identify areas for improvement, and refine goals and approaches.

4. Celebrating Success and Growth:
   - Recognition and Reward: Celebrating milestones, achievements, and personal growth accomplishments to reinforce motivation, build confidence, and sustain momentum.
   - Continuous Growth: Embracing a mindset of continuous improvement, ongoing learning, and personal development to maintain growth and achieve new aspirations.

By committing to personal growth, embracing challenges, setting actionable goals, and fostering a growth-oriented mindset, individuals can cultivate resilience, achieve fulfillment, and maximize their potential in various aspects of life. This chapter provides practical strategies and insights for embarking on a journey of self-improvement, goal achievement, and lifelong learning.

Chapter 31: Mindfulness and Presence

The Benefits of Mindfulness

The Wisdom of Discernment
Navigating Life's Good and Bad

Mindfulness involves cultivating present-moment awareness, focusing attention on the here and now without judgment, and fostering a sense of clarity, calmness, and acceptance.

1. Stress Reduction and Relaxation:
   - Stress Management: Practicing mindfulness techniques, such as deep breathing, meditation, or body scan exercises, to reduce stress, anxiety, and emotional reactivity.
   - Relaxation Response: Triggering the body's relaxation response through mindfulness practices to promote physical and mental relaxation.

2. Enhanced Emotional Regulation:
   - Emotional Awareness: Increasing awareness of thoughts, emotions, and bodily sensations to respond thoughtfully rather than react impulsively in challenging situations.
   - Self-compassion: Cultivating self-compassion and acceptance by embracing one's experiences, feelings, and imperfections with kindness and non-judgment.

3. Improved Concentration and Focus:
   - Attention Training: Strengthening attentional control and concentration through mindfulness exercises, enhancing productivity, and cognitive performance.
   - Mindful Work Practices: Applying mindfulness techniques to enhance focus, creativity, and problem-solving abilities in professional or academic settings.

4. Relationship Enhancement:
   - Empathy and Connection: Fostering empathy, active listening, and deeper connections with others through mindful communication and presence.
   - Conflict Resolution: Resolving conflicts or misunderstandings with mindful communication, understanding perspectives, and promoting mutual respect.

Techniques to Stay Present

Staying present involves practicing mindfulness techniques and integrating mindful awareness into daily routines to cultivate a state of presence and engagement with the present moment.

1. Mindful Breathing:
  - Diaphragmatic Breathing: Practicing deep, diaphragmatic breathing to anchor attention to the sensations of the breath, promoting relaxation and present-moment awareness.
  - Breath Awareness: Noticing the rhythm, depth, and sensations of each breath as it enters and leaves the body, fostering mindfulness and grounding in the present.

2. Body Scan Meditation:
  - Progressive Relaxation: Systematically scanning and relaxing different parts of the body from head to toe, heightening awareness of bodily sensations and promoting relaxation.
  - Body Awareness: Noticing physical sensations, tensions, or discomforts in the body without judgment, enhancing body-mind connection and mindful presence.

3. Mindful Observation:
  - Sensory Awareness: Engaging in mindful observation of surroundings, noticing sights, sounds, smells, textures, and tastes with curiosity and without attachment.
  - Nature Immersion: Connecting with nature through mindful walks, hikes, or outdoor activities to appreciate natural beauty, enhance sensory awareness, and promote relaxation.

4. Daily Mindfulness Practices:
  - Mindful Eating: Practicing mindful eating by savoring each bite, observing flavors, textures, and sensations, and cultivating appreciation for nourishing food choices.
  - Mindful Pause: Taking mindful breaks throughout the day to pause, breathe, and check in with present-moment experiences, promoting clarity, stress reduction, and renewed focus.

By integrating mindfulness into daily life, practicing present-moment awareness, and embracing mindful techniques, individuals can cultivate inner peace, resilience, and a deeper connection to themselves and the world around them. This chapter provides practical strategies and insights for experiencing the benefits of mindfulness and fostering a sense of presence and well-being in everyday experiences.

Chapter 32: The Role of Gratitude

Practicing Gratitude

The Wisdom of Discernment
Navigating Life's Good and Bad

Gratitude involves acknowledging and appreciating the positive aspects of life, experiences, and relationships, fostering a mindset of thankfulness and appreciation.

1. Daily Gratitude Practices:
   - Gratitude Journaling: Writing down three things each day that you are grateful for, reflecting on positive experiences, moments of joy, or acts of kindness.
   - Gratitude Rituals: Incorporating gratitude into daily routines, such as expressing thanks before meals, bedtime reflections, or morning affirmations.

2. Mindful Appreciation:
   - Savoring Moments: Taking time to fully experience and appreciate pleasant experiences, such as nature walks, meals, or meaningful conversations.
   - Gratitude Meditation: Practicing guided meditation focused on gratitude, cultivating feelings of warmth, appreciation, and connection with oneself and others.

3. Acts of Kindness and Giving:
   - Expressing Appreciation: Showing appreciation through acts of kindness, gestures, or words of gratitude towards others, fostering positive relationships and strengthening social connections.
   - Volunteerism: Engaging in volunteer activities or community service to contribute to the well-being of others and cultivate a sense of purpose and gratitude.

Its Effect on Perception and Well-being

Practicing gratitude positively influences perception, emotional well-being, and overall quality of life by cultivating a mindset of abundance, resilience, and happiness.

1. Emotional Resilience:
   - Positive Outlook: Enhancing resilience by focusing on the positive aspects of life, nurturing optimism, and coping effectively with challenges or setbacks.
   - Stress Reduction: Mitigating stress and anxiety through gratitude practices, promoting relaxation, emotional balance, and mental well-being.

2. Relationship Enhancement:

    - Building Connection: Strengthening interpersonal relationships by expressing appreciation, fostering trust, and deepening emotional bonds with family, friends, or colleagues.

    - Conflict Resolution: Facilitating conflict resolution and promoting forgiveness by acknowledging and appreciating others' strengths and contributions.

3. Physical Health Benefits:

    - Improved Sleep: Enhancing sleep quality and duration by cultivating a grateful mindset, reducing negative thought patterns, and promoting relaxation before bedtime.

    - Enhanced Immune Function: Boosting immune system function and overall health by reducing stress hormones and promoting a positive emotional state through gratitude practices.

4. Personal Growth and Fulfillment:

    - Self-esteem and Confidence: Increasing self-esteem and self-worth by recognizing personal strengths, achievements, and blessings through gratitude reflection.

    - Sense of Purpose: Cultivating a sense of purpose and fulfillment by appreciating life's blessings, experiences, and opportunities for growth and contribution.

By integrating gratitude into daily life, practicing mindful appreciation, and acknowledging the positive aspects of life, individuals can enhance emotional well-being, foster resilience, and cultivate a deeper sense of fulfillment and connection with themselves and others. This chapter provides practical strategies and insights for incorporating gratitude practices into daily routines and experiencing the transformative effects on perception and overall well-being.

Chapter 33: Spiritual Discernment

Exploring Spiritual Practices

The Wisdom of Discernment

Navigating Life's Good and Bad

Spiritual discernment involves seeking clarity, wisdom, and guidance through spiritual practices that nurture a deeper connection with oneself, others, and the divine.

1. Meditation and Contemplation:
   - Mindfulness Meditation: Engaging in mindfulness practices to cultivate present-moment awareness, inner peace, and spiritual growth.
   - Contemplative Prayer: Reflecting deeply on spiritual teachings, scriptures, or personal beliefs to deepen understanding and connection with spiritual principles.

2. Sacred Rituals and Ceremonies:
   - Rituals of Worship: Participating in religious or spiritual rituals, ceremonies, or worship services that foster spiritual connection, community, and reverence.
   - Sacred Spaces: Creating or visiting sacred spaces, such as temples, churches, or natural environments, to cultivate a sense of awe, reverence, and spiritual presence.

3. Study and Reflection:
   - Scripture Study: Studying religious texts, spiritual teachings, or philosophical writings to gain insight, wisdom, and spiritual guidance.
   - Personal Reflection: Reflecting on personal experiences, values, beliefs, and moral principles to deepen spiritual awareness and discernment.

Finding Spiritual Balance

Finding spiritual balance involves integrating spiritual practices, values, and beliefs into daily life to promote inner harmony, purpose, and alignment with higher principles.

1. Alignment with Core Values:
   - Identifying Core Beliefs: Clarifying personal beliefs, values, and principles that guide ethical decision-making, behavior, and spiritual growth.
   - Living with Integrity: Aligning actions, choices, and relationships with spiritual values and principles to promote authenticity and moral integrity.

2. Service and Compassion:

- Acts of Service: Engaging in compassionate acts of service, volunteerism, or philanthropy to contribute to the well-being of others and foster spiritual fulfillment.

- Empathy and Understanding: Cultivating empathy, compassion, and understanding towards others' experiences, challenges, and spiritual journeys.

3. Spiritual Guidance and Mentorship:

- Seeking Spiritual Counsel: Consulting spiritual mentors, advisors, or community leaders for guidance, support, and wisdom on spiritual matters.

- Peer Support: Participating in spiritual communities, study groups, or support networks to share insights, experiences, and spiritual growth journeys.

4. Integration of Mind, Body, and Spirit:

- Holistic Well-being: Nurturing holistic well-being by integrating physical health, emotional balance, and spiritual practices to promote overall vitality and harmony.

- Mind-Body Practices: Incorporating mind-body practices, such as yoga, tai chi, or qigong, to cultivate inner peace, balance, and spiritual awareness.

By exploring spiritual practices, seeking spiritual balance, and aligning with core values and beliefs, individuals can deepen their spiritual discernment, cultivate inner peace, and foster a sense of purpose and connection with the divine and the world around them. This chapter provides practical strategies and insights for integrating spiritual principles into daily life and nurturing a meaningful and fulfilling spiritual journey.

Chapter 34: Handling Uncertainty

Strategies for Navigating the Unknown

Handling uncertainty involves developing adaptive strategies, cultivating resilience, and embracing uncertainty as an opportunity for growth and learning.

1. Mindful Awareness:

- Acceptance of Uncertainty: Embracing uncertainty as a natural part of life and cultivating mindfulness practices to stay present, calm, and resilient in uncertain situations.

- Flexible Thinking: Adopting a flexible mindset, open to new possibilities and alternative solutions, to navigate unpredictable circumstances effectively.

2. Coping Mechanisms:

- Stress Management: Employing stress reduction techniques, such as deep breathing, meditation, or physical exercise, to manage anxiety and maintain emotional balance during uncertain times.

- Problem-Solving Skills: Developing problem-solving skills and critical thinking abilities to analyze challenges, explore options, and make informed decisions in uncertain situations.

3. Seeking Support and Guidance:

- Social Support: Engaging with trusted friends, family members, or support networks to seek emotional support, perspective, and encouragement during periods of uncertainty.

- Professional Advice: Consulting mentors, advisors, or experts in relevant fields for guidance, advice, and expertise to navigate complex or unfamiliar situations effectively.

Building Resilience

Building resilience involves strengthening mental, emotional, and physical resources to adapt, cope, and thrive in the face of adversity, setbacks, or uncertainty.

1. Self-care Practices:

- Physical Well-being: Prioritizing physical health, nutrition, sleep, and exercise to enhance resilience, energy levels, and overall well-being.

- Emotional Regulation: Practicing emotional self-awareness, self-compassion, and positive coping strategies to manage stress and maintain emotional stability.

2. Adaptive Coping Strategies:

- Problem-focused Coping: Taking proactive steps to address challenges, break down tasks into manageable steps, and develop action plans to achieve goals despite uncertainty.

- Emotion-focused Coping: Using strategies such as relaxation techniques, journaling, or artistic expression to process emotions, reduce stress, and foster emotional resilience.

The Wisdom of Discernment
Navigating Life's Good and Bad

3. Learning and Growth Mindset:
  - Continuous Learning: Embracing a growth mindset by seeking opportunities for learning, skill development, and personal growth to adapt to changing circumstances and challenges.
  - Resilient Thinking: Cultivating optimistic thinking, resilience-building beliefs, and reframing challenges as opportunities for learning, growth, and personal development.

4. Cultivating Purpose and Meaning:
  - Values Alignment: Aligning actions, decisions, and goals with personal values, purpose, and long-term aspirations to maintain motivation and resilience during uncertain times.
  - Finding Meaning: Finding meaning and purpose in experiences, relationships, and contributions to foster resilience, inner strength, and a sense of fulfillment.

By implementing strategies for navigating uncertainty, building resilience, and embracing growth-oriented mindsets, individuals can effectively cope with challenges, adapt to change, and thrive in unpredictable environments. This chapter provides practical insights and tools for developing resilience, managing uncertainty, and cultivating a resilient mindset for personal and professional success.

Chapter 35: Influence of Media

Evaluating Media Messages

The influence of media encompasses the messages, narratives, and information disseminated through various forms of media, shaping perceptions, attitudes, and behaviors of individuals and society.

1. Critical Consumption:
  - Media Literacy: Developing critical thinking skills to analyze and evaluate media messages, sources, biases, and intentions.
  - Fact-checking: Verifying information from multiple credible sources to discern factual accuracy and reliability of media content.

2. Recognizing Bias and Agenda:

- Identifying Bias: Recognizing implicit and explicit biases in media content, including political, social, cultural, or commercial biases that may influence perspectives.

- Agenda-setting: Understanding the agenda-setting function of media in prioritizing certain issues, topics, or narratives to shape public opinion and discourse.

3. Media Representation:

- Diverse Perspectives: Advocating for diverse representation and inclusive portrayal of individuals, communities, and social issues in media content.

- Stereotype Awareness: Challenging stereotypes, misrepresentations, or harmful portrayals perpetuated by media and promoting accurate, nuanced depictions.

Making Informed Choices

Making informed choices involves conscientious consumption, active engagement, and responsible use of media to promote informed decision-making and critical engagement.

1. Media Consumption Habits:

- Selective Exposure: Being mindful of media consumption habits, preferences, and exposure to diverse viewpoints, perspectives, and genres.

- Balanced Information Intake: Seeking balanced information from reputable sources, including alternative viewpoints and credible analysis, to avoid echo chambers.

2. Ethical Considerations:

- Media Ethics: Understanding ethical principles and standards in journalism, advertising, and media production to uphold integrity, transparency, and accountability.

- Responsible Sharing: Exercising discretion and responsibility when sharing media content, ensuring accuracy, context, and potential impact on others.

3. Digital Literacy and Safety:

- Cybersecurity Awareness: Practicing cybersecurity measures to protect personal data, privacy, and digital identities while navigating online media platforms.

- Critical Engagement: Engaging critically with social media, digital platforms, and online communities to evaluate information credibility, combat misinformation, and promote digital literacy.

4. Media Impact on Society:
   - Cultural Influence: Recognizing the cultural, social, and political impacts of media on attitudes, beliefs, and societal norms.
   - Media Effects: Understanding how media consumption influences behaviors, perceptions, and public discourse, including its role in shaping public opinion and policy.

By cultivating media literacy skills, engaging critically with media content, and making informed choices, individuals can navigate the complex landscape of media influence, promote ethical media practices, and contribute to informed public discourse and decision-making. This chapter provides practical strategies and insights for evaluating media messages, making responsible media choices, and fostering media literacy in everyday life.

Chapter 36: Recognizing True Friendship

Characteristics of Genuine Friends

True friendship is marked by authentic connections, mutual respect, support, and loyalty, fostering meaningful relationships that enrich personal growth and well-being.

1. Trust and Reliability:
   - Trustworthiness: Demonstrating honesty, integrity, and reliability in words and actions, fostering a sense of trust and security in the friendship.
   - Dependability: Being consistent, dependable, and present during times of need or adversity, offering support and reassurance.

2. Empathy and Understanding:
   - Empathetic Listening: Listening actively and empathetically, understanding and validating each other's feelings, perspectives, and experiences.

- Compassionate Support: Offering emotional support, comfort, and encouragement without judgment or criticism, demonstrating care and understanding.

3. Respect and Acceptance:
  - Respectful Boundaries: Respecting personal boundaries, beliefs, and differences while celebrating each other's uniqueness and individuality.
  - Non-judgmental Acceptance: Accepting each other unconditionally, embracing strengths, weaknesses, and imperfections without expectation of perfection.

4. Mutual Support and Encouragement:
  - Shared Values: Sharing common values, interests, and goals, aligning mutual aspirations and supporting each other's personal and professional growth.
  - Celebrating Successes: Celebrating achievements, milestones, and successes together, fostering a culture of encouragement and mutual celebration.

Building Lasting Friendships

Building lasting friendships requires nurturing, communication, and mutual investment in maintaining positive, supportive, and enduring relationships.

1. Open Communication:
  - Honest Dialogue: Communicating openly and honestly, addressing conflicts or misunderstandings promptly, and resolving differences respectfully.
  - Active Engagement: Engaging in meaningful conversations, shared activities, and quality time together to strengthen bonds and deepen connection.

2. Reciprocity and Generosity:
  - Reciprocal Giving: Offering mutual support, kindness, and generosity, reciprocating acts of care, thoughtfulness, and consideration.
  - Shared Experiences: Creating memories through shared experiences, adventures, and moments of joy, fostering a sense of camaraderie and belonging.

3. Sustaining Long-distance Friendships:

- Regular Communication: Maintaining regular communication through calls, messages, or video chats to stay connected despite geographical distance.
   - Virtual Gatherings: Organizing virtual gatherings, online activities, or reunions to strengthen bonds and nurture friendships over time.

4. Conflict Resolution and Forgiveness:
   - Resolving Conflicts: Addressing conflicts constructively, listening actively, and seeking mutual understanding to preserve trust and harmony in the friendship.
   - Forgiveness and Reconciliation: Practicing forgiveness, letting go of grievances, and reconciling differences to rebuild and strengthen the friendship bond.

By recognizing the characteristics of genuine friendship, investing in mutual trust and support, and nurturing lasting connections through communication and shared experiences, individuals can cultivate meaningful friendships that contribute to personal happiness, resilience, and fulfillment. This chapter provides practical insights and strategies for identifying true friendship, building and sustaining lasting relationships, and navigating challenges to strengthen bonds of companionship and support.

Chapter 37: Love and Affection

Understanding Different Forms of Love

Love encompasses diverse expressions, emotions, and relationships, fostering deep connections and emotional bonds that enrich personal experiences and well-being.

1. Romantic Love:
   - Passion and Intimacy: Experiencing romantic attraction, emotional intimacy, and physical affection in committed relationships or partnerships.
   - Companionship: Sharing companionship, mutual support, and shared aspirations with a romantic partner, fostering a deep emotional connection and partnership.

2. Familial Love:

The Wisdom of Discernment
Navigating Life's Good and Bad

- Unconditional Bond: Nurturing unconditional love, support, and acceptance within family relationships, including parents, siblings, and extended family members.

- Generational Connection: Celebrating family traditions, values, and cultural heritage, fostering a sense of belonging and shared identity.

3. Friendship Love:

- Companionship and Trust: Cultivating meaningful friendships based on trust, mutual respect, and shared interests, offering emotional support and companionship.

- Shared Experiences: Creating lasting memories, laughter, and support through shared experiences, adventures, and life milestones.

4. Self-love and Compassion:

- Self-acceptance: Practicing self-love, self-compassion, and self-care, nurturing a positive self-image, and fostering inner peace and emotional well-being.

- Personal Growth: Embracing personal growth, resilience, and self-discovery through self-reflection, forgiveness, and embracing one's strengths and imperfections.

Healthy Expressions of Affection

Healthy expressions of affection involve genuine care, respect, and emotional connection, promoting mutual understanding, and nurturing positive relationships.

1. Verbal Affirmation:

- Words of Affirmation: Expressing love, appreciation, and admiration through verbal affirmations, compliments, and heartfelt messages.

- Encouraging Communication: Communicating openly, honestly, and respectfully to express feelings, needs, and desires in relationships.

2. Physical Affection:

- Physical Touch: Demonstrating affection and closeness through hugs, kisses, hand-holding, or comforting gestures, fostering emotional connection and intimacy.

- Respecting Boundaries: Respecting personal boundaries, preferences, and comfort levels when expressing physical affection, ensuring mutual consent and comfort.

3. Acts of Service:

   - Thoughtful Gestures: Showing love and consideration through acts of service, such as helping, supporting, or assisting loved ones in practical ways.

   - Shared Responsibilities: Collaborating and sharing responsibilities in relationships, demonstrating commitment, and building mutual trust and support.

4. Quality Time:

   - Focused Attention: Spending quality time together, engaging in meaningful conversations, shared activities, or adventures to nurture emotional connection and intimacy.

   - Creating Memories: Creating lasting memories and experiences through shared interests, hobbies, or special moments that strengthen bonds and deepen relationships.

By understanding the diverse forms of love, cultivating healthy expressions of affection, and fostering emotional connection and understanding in relationships, individuals can nurture meaningful connections, promote emotional well-being, and experience the transformative power of love in their lives. This chapter provides practical insights and strategies for embracing love, expressing affection, and fostering positive relationships that contribute to personal happiness, fulfillment, and resilience.

Chapter 38: Personal Accountability

Owning Your Actions

Personal accountability involves taking responsibility for your choices, behaviors, and decisions, fostering integrity, trustworthiness, and self-improvement.

1. Self-awareness and Reflection:

   - Acknowledging Mistakes: Recognizing and accepting responsibility for mistakes, errors, or shortcomings without excuses or blame-shifting.

   - Learning from Experience: Reflecting on past actions, decisions, and outcomes to gain insights, learn lessons, and make informed choices in the future.

The Wisdom of Discernment
Navigating Life's Good and Bad

2. Integrity and Honesty:

  - Aligning Actions with Values: Acting in accordance with personal values, ethical principles, and moral standards to maintain integrity and credibility.

  - Transparent Communication: Communicating openly and honestly, sharing information, intentions, and commitments with clarity and sincerity.

3. Setting and Achieving Goals:

  - Goal Clarity: Setting clear, achievable goals and objectives, establishing action plans, and taking proactive steps to achieve desired outcomes.

  - Accountability Partnerships: Engaging in accountability partnerships or support networks to stay focused, motivated, and accountable for personal and professional goals.

4. Resilience and Adaptability:

  - Handling Adversity: Responding resiliently to challenges, setbacks, or obstacles, taking ownership of responses, and seeking constructive solutions.

  - Flexibility and Adaptation: Adapting to change, adjusting plans or strategies as needed, and maintaining a proactive mindset in dynamic environments.

Encouraging Accountability in Others

Encouraging accountability in others involves fostering a culture of responsibility, transparency, and mutual support in personal and professional relationships.

1. Setting Clear Expectations:

  - Defining Roles and Responsibilities: Clarifying roles, expectations, and deliverables in team settings or collaborative projects to promote clarity and accountability.

  - Agreed-upon Standards: Establishing shared goals, benchmarks, or performance standards to measure progress and ensure accountability.

2. Effective Communication:

  - Constructive Feedback: Providing constructive feedback, guidance, and mentorship to empower others to take ownership of their actions and outcomes.

- Active Listening: Listening attentively to others' perspectives, concerns, or challenges, demonstrating empathy and understanding in accountability discussions.

3. Supporting Growth and Development:
  - Coaching and Mentorship: Offering guidance, resources, or developmental opportunities to help others enhance skills, capabilities, and accountability.
  - Recognition and Celebration: Acknowledging and celebrating achievements, milestones, or improvements to reinforce accountability and foster a culture of success.

4. Promoting Collaboration and Teamwork:
  - Collaborative Problem-solving: Encouraging teamwork, collaboration, and collective accountability to address challenges, innovate solutions, and achieve shared goals.
  - Shared Ownership: Cultivating a sense of shared ownership, responsibility, and pride in collective achievements, fostering a positive and supportive work environment.

By embracing personal accountability, fostering integrity, and encouraging accountability in others, individuals can cultivate a culture of responsibility, trust, and achievement in personal and professional settings. This chapter provides practical strategies and insights for taking ownership of actions, promoting transparency, and empowering others to embrace accountability for mutual growth and success.

Chapter 39: Courage and Vulnerability

The Interplay Between Courage and Vulnerability

Courage and vulnerability are intertwined aspects of personal growth, resilience, and emotional authenticity, shaping how individuals navigate challenges, relationships, and self-discovery.

1. Courage as a Catalyst:
  - Facing Fears: Confronting fears, uncertainties, and adversities with courage, resilience, and determination to overcome obstacles and achieve personal goals.

The Wisdom of Discernment

Navigating Life's Good and Bad

- Taking Initiative: Initiating action, making bold decisions, and stepping outside comfort zones to pursue opportunities for growth and fulfillment.

2. Vulnerability as Strength:
  - Authentic Expression: Embracing vulnerability as a pathway to authenticity, openness, and emotional honesty in relationships, fostering deeper connections and trust.
  - Self-acceptance: Accepting imperfections, insecurities, and emotional struggles as integral parts of personal identity and growth, promoting self-compassion and resilience.

3. Emotional Resilience:
  - Adapting to Change: Embracing vulnerability as a catalyst for adaptation, flexibility, and learning from experiences to build emotional resilience and strength.
  - Seeking Support: Seeking support, guidance, or reassurance from trusted individuals or support networks during times of vulnerability, fostering emotional well-being and growth.

Embracing Both in Life

Embracing both courage and vulnerability involves cultivating a balanced approach to personal development, relationships, and navigating life's challenges with authenticity and resilience.

1. Self-discovery and Growth:
  - Exploring New Horizons: Embracing vulnerability to explore new opportunities, experiences, and perspectives that promote personal growth and self-discovery.
  - Learning from Setbacks: Learning from setbacks, failures, or disappointments with courage, resilience, and a growth-oriented mindset to foster continuous improvement.

2. Building Meaningful Connections:
  - Authentic Relationships: Building meaningful connections and deepening relationships through genuine communication, empathy, and mutual vulnerability.
  - Trust and Intimacy: Cultivating trust, intimacy, and emotional bonds in relationships by embracing vulnerability as a foundation for shared understanding and support.

3. Empowerment and Impact:

- Empowering Others: Inspiring and empowering others through acts of courage, vulnerability, and authenticity, fostering a supportive and inclusive community.

- Making a Difference: Contributing positively to society, advocating for change, and addressing societal challenges with courage, empathy, and a commitment to social justice.

4. Self-care and Resilience:

- Balancing Strength and Sensitivity: Balancing strength and sensitivity by practicing self-care, setting boundaries, and prioritizing emotional well-being amidst challenges.

- Seeking Balance: Striving for balance between courage and vulnerability in decision-making, actions, and relationships to foster personal fulfillment and resilience.

By embracing courage and vulnerability as complementary forces in personal growth, relationships, and life experiences, individuals can cultivate resilience, authenticity, and meaningful connections that contribute to personal happiness, fulfillment, and positive impact in the world. This chapter provides practical insights and strategies for navigating challenges, embracing authenticity, and fostering emotional well-being through courage and vulnerability.

Chapter 40: Balance and Harmony

Achieving Life Balance

Life balance involves harmonizing various aspects of life—such as work, relationships, health, and personal growth—to promote well-being, fulfillment, and sustainable success.

1. Identifying Priorities:

- Setting Priorities: Identifying core values, goals, and priorities to allocate time, energy, and resources effectively across different areas of life.

- Balanced Perspective: Maintaining a holistic view of life and considering the interconnectedness of physical, emotional, mental, and spiritual well-being.

2. Time Management and Boundaries:

The Wisdom of Discernment

Navigating Life's Good and Bad

- Effective Time Management: Prioritizing tasks, activities, and commitments based on importance and urgency, while also scheduling time for rest, relaxation, and personal interests.

- Setting Boundaries: Establishing clear boundaries in personal and professional relationships to manage expectations, reduce stress, and preserve balance.

3. Well-being and Self-care:

- Holistic Health: Nurturing physical health through regular exercise, nutritious eating habits, and adequate sleep to sustain energy levels and overall well-being.

- Emotional Resilience: Cultivating emotional resilience through stress management techniques, mindfulness practices, and seeking support from trusted individuals or resources.

4. Continuous Learning and Growth:

- Lifelong Learning: Pursuing opportunities for personal and professional development, acquiring new skills, knowledge, and perspectives to adapt to changing circumstances.

- Adaptability: Embracing flexibility and adaptability in navigating life transitions, challenges, and opportunities with resilience and a growth-oriented mindset.

The Importance of Harmony

Harmony encompasses the alignment, coherence, and integration of diverse elements within oneself and one's environment, fostering peace, fulfillment, and positive relationships.

1. Inner Harmony:

- Self-awareness: Cultivating self-awareness, introspection, and mindfulness practices to achieve inner peace, clarity, and emotional balance.

- Integration of Values: Aligning actions, decisions, and behaviors with personal values, beliefs, and aspirations to promote authenticity and integrity.

2. Interpersonal Harmony:

- Effective Communication: Fostering open, honest, and empathetic communication in relationships, promoting mutual understanding, trust, and harmony.

- Collaboration and Cooperation: Engaging in collaborative efforts, teamwork, and shared goals to build supportive networks and nurturing connections.

3. Environmental Harmony:

- Sustainability: Supporting environmental sustainability efforts, responsible consumption practices, and eco-friendly initiatives to preserve natural resources and promote planetary well-being.

- Community Engagement: Contributing positively to local communities, promoting social justice, inclusivity, and fostering a sense of belonging and collective harmony.

4. Achieving Fulfillment:

- Meaningful Engagement: Participating in activities, pursuits, and endeavors that align with personal passions, interests, and values, fostering a sense of purpose and fulfillment.

- Balance and Satisfaction: Striving for balance, satisfaction, and contentment in life by honoring individual needs, aspirations, and contributions to society.

By striving for life balance and cultivating harmony within oneself, relationships, and environment, individuals can enhance well-being, resilience, and holistic fulfillment. This chapter provides practical insights and strategies for achieving life balance, fostering harmony, and promoting personal and collective well-being in diverse aspects of life.

Chapter 41: Living with Integrity

Defining Integrity

Integrity is the quality of being honest, ethical, and consistent in thoughts, words, and actions, aligning with moral principles, values, and beliefs.

1. Honesty and Truthfulness:

- Truthfulness: Speaking the truth and being transparent in communications, interactions, and relationships, fostering trust and credibility.

- Authenticity: Embracing authenticity and sincerity in expressing thoughts, feelings, and intentions without deception or manipulation.

2. Ethical Decision-making:
  - Ethical Standards: Upholding ethical standards, moral values, and principles in decision-making processes, actions, and behaviors.
  - Accountability: Taking responsibility for choices, behaviors, and outcomes, demonstrating accountability and integrity in personal and professional contexts.

3. Consistency and Reliability:
  - Reliability: Being dependable, consistent, and trustworthy in fulfilling commitments, obligations, and promises made to oneself and others.
  - Alignment with Values: Ensuring actions and behaviors align with core values, beliefs, and principles, even in challenging or uncertain circumstances.

Living a Life True to Your Values

Living a life true to your values involves aligning actions, decisions, and behaviors with personal beliefs, principles, and aspirations to promote authenticity, fulfillment, and meaningful impact.

1. Identifying Core Values:
  - Self-reflection: Engaging in self-reflection and introspection to identify and prioritize core values that guide beliefs, attitudes, and behaviors.
  - Clarity of Purpose: Clarifying personal purpose, goals, and intentions aligned with values to foster clarity and direction in life choices.

2. Making Ethical Choices:
  - Integrity in Action: Applying ethical principles and values in decision-making processes, honoring commitments, and upholding moral integrity in all aspects of life.
  - Resisting Temptations: Resisting temptations or pressures that compromise integrity, demonstrating resilience and strength of character in challenging situations.

3. Building Trust and Respect:

- Trustworthiness: Building trust and respect through consistent, ethical conduct, reliability, and accountability in personal and professional relationships.

- Honoring Commitments: Fulfilling promises, agreements, and responsibilities with integrity, demonstrating respect for oneself and others' trust.

4. Cultivating Integrity Daily:

- Daily Practices: Integrating integrity into daily practices, interactions, and decisions to foster a culture of honesty, fairness, and ethical behavior.

- Continuous Improvement: Committing to continuous self-improvement, learning, and growth to strengthen integrity and uphold values-driven actions.

By defining integrity, living a life true to personal values, and embodying ethical principles in daily actions and decisions, individuals can cultivate authenticity, trustworthiness, and positive influence in their personal and professional lives. This chapter provides practical insights and strategies for embracing integrity as a guiding principle for personal growth, ethical conduct, and meaningful contributions to society

Chapter 42: Cultivating Joy

Finding Joy in Everyday Life

Joy is a deep-seated sense of happiness and contentment that transcends momentary pleasures, rooted in gratitude, mindfulness, and positive experiences.

1. Practicing Gratitude:

- Gratitude Journaling: Keeping a gratitude journal to reflect on and appreciate daily blessings, experiences, and moments of joy.

- Mindful Awareness: Practicing mindfulness to savor the present moment, notice beauty in everyday life, and cultivate a sense of gratitude and contentment.

2. Embracing Positivity:

- Positive Mindset: Cultivating a positive outlook on life, focusing on strengths, achievements, and possibilities rather than dwelling on challenges or setbacks.

- Optimism: Embracing optimism and resilience in facing adversity, maintaining hope, and seeking opportunities for growth and learning.

3. Finding Fulfillment:

 - Purposeful Living: Engaging in activities, pursuits, and relationships that align with personal values, passions, and interests to foster fulfillment and joy.

 - Self-care: Prioritizing self-care practices, hobbies, and activities that promote relaxation, rejuvenation, and emotional well-being.

Sharing Joy with Others

Sharing joy with others involves spreading positivity, kindness, and compassion, fostering connections, and contributing to collective happiness and well-being.

1. Acts of Kindness:

 - Random Acts of Kindness: Performing random acts of kindness, generosity, and compassion toward others to uplift spirits and create positive ripple effects.

 - Volunteering and Service: Contributing time, skills, or resources to support charitable causes, community initiatives, or individuals in need.

2. Celebrating Success and Milestones:

 - Shared Achievements: Celebrating personal and collective achievements, milestones, and successes with loved ones, colleagues, or community members.

 - Creating Shared Memories: Creating memorable experiences, gatherings, or events that promote joy, laughter, and connection among participants.

3. Building Meaningful Relationships:

 - Connection and Support: Nurturing meaningful relationships based on trust, empathy, and mutual respect, offering emotional support and companionship.

 - Shared Experiences: Sharing moments of joy, laughter, and shared interests with friends, family, or peers to strengthen bonds and create lasting memories.

4. Spreading Positivity:

- Positive Influence: Being a source of encouragement, inspiration, and positivity in interactions with others, uplifting spirits and promoting well-being.
- Cultivating a Joyful Environment: Creating and contributing to environments, workplaces, or communities that foster joy, creativity, and a sense of belonging.

By cultivating joy in everyday life, embracing positivity, and sharing moments of happiness and kindness with others, individuals can enhance their well-being, strengthen relationships, and contribute to a more joyful and compassionate world. This chapter provides practical insights and strategies for finding joy, spreading positivity, and creating meaningful connections that enrich personal happiness and collective well-being.

Chapter 43: Navigating Loss and Grief

Understanding the Grieving Process

Grief is a natural response to loss, encompassing emotional, physical, and psychological reactions that vary in intensity and duration, characterized by stages of mourning and adaptation.

1. Stages of Grief:
  - Denial: Initially refusing to accept the reality of loss, feeling shock, numbness, or disbelief.
  - Anger: Experiencing frustration, resentment, or anger toward oneself, others, or the situation.
  - Bargaining: Seeking ways to negotiate or reverse the loss, making promises or seeking solutions to alleviate pain.
  - Depression: Feeling deep sadness, emptiness, or despair as the reality of loss sets in.
  - Acceptance: Achieving a gradual acceptance of the loss, adapting to a new reality, and finding a sense of peace or resolution.

2. Emotional Responses:
  - Sadness and Sorrow: Feeling overwhelming sadness, sorrow, or emotional pain in response to the absence or change caused by loss.

The Wisdom of Discernment
Navigating Life's Good and Bad

   - Guilt and Regret: Experiencing guilt, regret, or self-blame over perceived actions, words, or decisions related to the loss.
   - Anxiety and Fear: Feeling anxious, fearful, or uncertain about the future and adjusting to life without the presence of what or whom is lost.

3. Physical and Behavioral Reactions:
   - Fatigue and Exhaustion: Experiencing physical fatigue, exhaustion, or changes in appetite, sleep patterns, or energy levels.
   - Withdrawal and Isolation: Withdrawing from social activities or relationships, needing time alone to process emotions and cope with grief.
   - Physical Symptoms: Experiencing physical symptoms such as headaches, stomachaches, or muscle tension due to stress and emotional strain.

 Finding Healing

Finding healing involves navigating grief with compassion, self-care, and support, embracing coping strategies, and honoring the memory of what or whom is lost.

1. Self-compassion and Patience:
   - Self-care Practices: Engaging in self-care activities that promote emotional and physical well-being, such as exercise, rest, and relaxation techniques.
   - Accepting Emotions: Allowing oneself to experience and express a range of emotions without judgment or pressure to "move on" too quickly.

2. Seeking Support:
   - Social Support: Connecting with friends, family members, or support groups who can offer empathy, understanding, and companionship during the grieving process.
   - Professional Help: Seeking guidance from therapists, counselors, or grief support specialists to process emotions, gain perspective, and develop coping strategies.

3. Honoring Memories:
   - Rituals and Tributes: Creating rituals, ceremonies, or tributes to honor and commemorate the life, achievements, and impact of what or whom is lost.

- Legacy and Meaning: Finding meaning and purpose in preserving the legacy, values, and memories associated with the loss through storytelling, keepsakes, or charitable contributions.

4. Navigating Life Transitions:
   - Adjusting to Change: Recognizing and adapting to life changes, roles, or responsibilities resulting from the loss, seeking stability, and finding new sources of fulfillment.
   - Finding Hope and Resilience: Cultivating hope, resilience, and a sense of purpose in moving forward while cherishing the memories and lessons learned from the loss experience.

By understanding the grieving process, embracing healing practices, and seeking support from others, individuals can navigate loss with resilience, compassion, and eventual acceptance, honoring the memory of what or whom is lost while finding strength and hope for the future. This chapter provides practical insights and strategies for coping with grief, finding healing, and integrating loss into personal growth and resilience.

Chapter 44: Adaptability and Change

Embracing Change

Change is an inevitable part of life, encompassing transitions, challenges, and opportunities that require flexibility, resilience, and a growth-oriented mindset.

1. Understanding Change:
   - Nature of Change: Recognizing change as a constant and dynamic force that shapes personal, professional, and societal landscapes.
   - Impact of Change: Acknowledging the emotional, psychological, and practical effects of change on individuals, relationships, and communities.

2. Mindset and Perspective:
   - Growth Mindset: Embracing a growth-oriented mindset that views change as an opportunity for learning, self-improvement, and adaptation.

The Wisdom of Discernment
Navigating Life's Good and Bad

- Optimism: Cultivating optimism and resilience to navigate uncertainty, setbacks, and challenges associated with change.

3. Embracing New Opportunities:
- Exploring Possibilities: Embracing change as a catalyst for exploring new opportunities, experiences, and perspectives that promote personal growth and development.
- Creativity and Innovation: Harnessing creativity and innovation to adapt to changing circumstances, solve problems, and seize new opportunities for advancement.

Strategies for Adaptation

Adaptability involves adjusting to new circumstances, environments, or expectations with flexibility, creativity, and proactive strategies to thrive amidst change.

1. Flexibility and Openness:
- Adapting to Situations: Demonstrating flexibility and openness to new ideas, approaches, or roles in response to evolving circumstances or challenges.
- Resilience: Building resilience by maintaining a positive attitude, managing stress effectively, and bouncing back from setbacks or obstacles.

2. Continuous Learning and Skill Development:
- Lifelong Learning: Pursuing continuous learning, skill development, and personal growth to remain relevant, adaptable, and competitive in a changing world.
- Adaptive Skills: Developing adaptive skills, such as problem-solving, critical thinking, and emotional intelligence, to navigate complex and uncertain environments.

3. Effective Communication and Collaboration:
- Clear Communication: Communicating openly, transparently, and effectively with others to foster understanding, collaboration, and mutual support during times of change.
- Teamwork and Collaboration: Engaging in teamwork, collaboration, and collective problem-solving to leverage diverse perspectives, skills, and strengths in achieving shared goals.

The Wisdom of Discernment
Navigating Life's Good and Bad

4. Seeking Support and Feedback:

   - Seeking Guidance: Seeking guidance, feedback, or mentorship from trusted individuals, mentors, or professional networks to gain insights, perspective, and support in adapting to change.

   - Building Networks: Building and maintaining supportive networks, relationships, and communities that provide encouragement, resources, and opportunities for growth and adaptation.

By embracing change with a positive mindset, proactive strategies for adaptation, and a commitment to continuous learning and growth, individuals can navigate transitions, seize new opportunities, and thrive in dynamic and evolving environments. This chapter provides practical insights and strategies for embracing change, fostering adaptability, and harnessing resilience to achieve personal and professional success.

Chapter 45: Learning from Mistakes

The Role of Failure in Growth

Failure is a natural part of life and a valuable opportunity for learning, resilience, and personal development, shaping individuals' journeys toward success and fulfillment.

1. Embracing Failure as a Learning Opportunity:

   - Resilience Building: Developing resilience by navigating setbacks, challenges, and disappointments as opportunities for growth and self-improvement.

   - Learning Mindset: Cultivating a learning mindset that views failure as a stepping stone toward acquiring new skills, insights, and experiences.

2. Overcoming Fear of Failure:

   - Risk-taking: Embracing calculated risks and stepping outside comfort zones to pursue goals, innovation, and personal aspirations.

   - Perseverance: Demonstrating perseverance, determination, and grit in overcoming obstacles, setbacks, or failures on the path to success.

The Wisdom of Discernment
Navigating Life's Good and Bad

3. Personal Growth and Development:
   - Self-awareness: Reflecting on personal strengths, weaknesses, and areas for improvement through introspection and self-assessment.
   - Adaptability: Embracing change, feedback, and constructive criticism to adapt behaviors, strategies, and approaches for continuous improvement.

Turning Mistakes into Lessons

Turning mistakes into lessons involves reflecting on experiences, extracting insights, and applying newfound knowledge to make informed decisions and achieve desired outcomes.

1. Reflecting on Mistakes:
   - Self-reflection: Engaging in introspection to analyze mistakes, identify contributing factors, and understand the implications for personal growth and development.
   - Ownership and Accountability: Taking ownership of mistakes, acknowledging responsibilities, and learning from errors to prevent recurrence and foster accountability.

2. Extracting Key Learnings:
   - Identifying Patterns: Recognizing recurring patterns, behaviors, or decisions that contribute to mistakes and exploring alternative approaches or solutions.
   - Problem-solving Skills: Developing critical thinking, problem-solving skills, and decision-making abilities to navigate challenges, setbacks, and unexpected outcomes effectively.

3. Applying Lessons Learned:
   - Adaptive Strategies: Implementing adaptive strategies, adjustments, or improvements based on lessons learned from past mistakes to achieve desired goals and outcomes.
   - Continuous Improvement: Committing to continuous learning, growth, and refinement of skills, knowledge, and practices to enhance personal and professional development.

4. Seeking Support and Guidance:
   - Mentorship and Feedback: Seeking mentorship, guidance, or constructive feedback from mentors, peers, or trusted advisors to gain perspective, insights, and support in learning from mistakes.

- Building Resilience: Building resilience, emotional intelligence, and coping mechanisms to effectively manage setbacks, challenges, and adversity encountered along the journey of personal and professional growth.

By embracing failure as a catalyst for learning, resilience, and personal development, individuals can leverage mistakes as opportunities to gain valuable insights, refine skills, and achieve long-term success and fulfillment. This chapter provides practical insights and strategies for navigating failures, extracting lessons, and fostering continuous improvement in personal and professional endeavors.

Chapter 46: Celebrating Success

Recognizing and Celebrating Achievements

Celebrating success involves acknowledging milestones, accomplishments, and personal victories to foster motivation, confidence, and a sense of fulfillment.

1. Acknowledging Milestones:
   - Setting Goals: Establishing clear, measurable goals and milestones to track progress and achievements in personal, academic, or professional endeavors.
   - Reflecting on Progress: Reflecting on individual growth, accomplishments, and milestones achieved along the journey toward desired outcomes.

2. Promoting Self-Appreciation:
   - Self-Acknowledgment: Practicing self-appreciation and acknowledging personal efforts, resilience, and dedication in overcoming challenges and achieving goals.
   - Celebrating Small Wins: Celebrating incremental successes, achievements, or milestones to maintain momentum and motivation throughout the journey.

3. Formal Recognition:
   - Public Acknowledgment: Receiving formal recognition, awards, or accolades from peers, mentors, or organizations for outstanding achievements, contributions, or leadership.

- Honoring Achievements: Participating in ceremonies, ceremonies, or events that commemorate accomplishments and highlight significant milestones in personal or professional life.

Sharing Success with Others

Sharing success involves fostering a spirit of collaboration, generosity, and gratitude by acknowledging the contributions of others and inspiring collective achievement.

1. Team Recognition:
   - Team Collaboration: Acknowledging and celebrating team efforts, collaboration, and contributions that contributed to achieving shared goals or project success.
   - Building Morale: Boosting team morale, camaraderie, and unity through shared celebrations, recognition, and appreciation of collective achievements.

2. Mentorship and Support:
   - Mentor Recognition: Recognizing mentors, coaches, or advisors who provided guidance, support, and encouragement throughout the journey of personal or professional growth.
   - Paying It Forward: Inspiring others by sharing success stories, lessons learned, and experiences to mentor, motivate, and empower individuals pursuing similar paths or aspirations.

3. Community Impact:
   - Giving Back: Contributing to communities, causes, or organizations through philanthropy, volunteerism, or initiatives that create positive social impact and inspire collective success.
   - Role Modeling: Serving as a role model and mentor within communities, organizations, or professional networks to empower others and promote a culture of success, resilience, and achievement.

4. Gratitude and Appreciation:
   - Expressing Gratitude: Expressing gratitude and appreciation to supporters, mentors, family members, friends, or colleagues who provided encouragement, guidance, and belief in one's potential.

- Celebrating Together: Celebrating success with loved ones, peers, or colleagues through gatherings, events, or activities that promote camaraderie, joy, and shared accomplishments.

By recognizing and celebrating achievements, sharing success with others, and promoting a culture of appreciation, collaboration, and gratitude, individuals can foster motivation, inspire collective achievement, and cultivate a supportive environment conducive to personal and professional growth. This chapter provides practical insights and strategies for celebrating success, acknowledging achievements, and inspiring others through shared accomplishments and contributions to communities and organizations

Chapter 47: The Impact of Legacy

Thinking About Your Legacy

Thinking about your legacy involves reflecting on the values, actions, and contributions that define your life's purpose and the lasting impact you wish to leave on others and future generations.

1. Clarifying Personal Values and Beliefs:
   - Self-reflection: Engaging in introspection to identify core values, principles, and beliefs that guide decisions, behaviors, and interactions with others.
   - Defining Purpose: Clarifying personal aspirations, goals, and aspirations aligned with your values to shape a purpose-driven life and legacy.

2. Identifying Long-Term Goals and Aspirations:
   - Setting Goals: Establishing long-term goals, aspirations, and milestones that reflect your vision for personal growth, achievement, and fulfillment.
   - Legacy Planning: Developing a strategic plan or vision statement that outlines desired contributions, impacts, or achievements to be remembered and valued by others.

Building a Positive Legacy

Building a positive legacy involves making intentional choices, fostering meaningful connections, and creating lasting impacts that contribute to personal fulfillment and collective well-being.

1. Impactful Contributions and Achievements:
  - Making a Difference: Engaging in meaningful activities, projects, or initiatives that create positive change, address societal needs, or improve quality of life for others.
  - Professional Excellence: Demonstrating dedication, integrity, and excellence in professional endeavors to leave a lasting mark through innovation, leadership, or industry influence.

2. Promoting Values-Based Leadership:
  - Ethical Leadership: Exemplifying ethical leadership principles, fostering trust, and inspiring others through integrity, accountability, and transparent communication.
  - Mentorship and Guidance: Mentoring others, sharing knowledge, and empowering future leaders to cultivate a legacy of mentorship, support, and professional development.

3. Nurturing Meaningful Relationships:
  - Building Connections: Cultivating authentic relationships, networks, and communities based on trust, respect, and collaboration to foster collective achievement and support.
  - Family and Community Bonds: Strengthening family ties, nurturing community engagement, and promoting unity through shared values, traditions, and experiences.

4. Commitment to Social Responsibility:
  - Philanthropy and Giving: Contributing time, resources, or expertise to charitable causes, social initiatives, or community development projects that promote equity, justice, and social responsibility.
  - Environmental Stewardship: Advocating for environmental conservation, sustainability practices, and responsible stewardship of natural resources to safeguard future generations' well-being.

By thinking critically about your legacy, aligning actions with values, and building a positive legacy through impactful contributions, ethical leadership, and nurturing meaningful relationships, individuals can create a lasting impact, inspire others, and leave a meaningful imprint on the world. This chapter provides practical insights and strategies for reflecting on your legacy, setting intentions for meaningful contributions, and cultivating a legacy of purpose, influence, and positive change.

Chapter 48: Empowering Others

Encouraging and Uplifting Others

Empowering others involves fostering a supportive environment, providing encouragement, and promoting personal growth and development to help individuals realize their potential and achieve their goals.

1. Supportive Encouragement:
   - Providing Positive Feedback: Offering constructive feedback, praise, and recognition to acknowledge achievements, efforts, and progress.
   - Motivating Words: Using encouraging words, affirmations, and inspirational messages to boost confidence, resilience, and motivation.

2. Facilitating Growth and Development:
   - Setting Goals: Collaborating with individuals to set clear, achievable goals that align with their aspirations and support personal or professional development.
   - Offering Guidance: Providing mentorship, advice, and guidance based on experience, expertise, and insights to navigate challenges and seize opportunities.

3. Creating Opportunities:
   - Promoting Access: Advocating for equal access to resources, opportunities, and networks that empower individuals to pursue education, career advancement, and personal aspirations.
   - Networking and Connections: Facilitating introductions, networking opportunities, and connections within communities, organizations, or industries to expand possibilities and foster growth.

The Ripple Effect of Empowerment

Empowerment creates a ripple effect of positive change, inspiring individuals to take action, contribute to their communities, and support others in achieving success and fulfillment.

1. Inspiring Leadership:
  - Leading by Example: Demonstrating leadership qualities, values, and behaviors that inspire trust, integrity, and commitment to empowering others.
   - Cultivating Future Leaders: Mentoring and developing emerging leaders to cultivate a legacy of leadership, empowerment, and positive influence.

2. Building Resilience and Confidence:
  - Encouraging Resilience: Nurturing resilience, perseverance, and adaptability to navigate challenges, setbacks, and obstacles with confidence and determination.
   - Celebrating Diversity: Embracing diversity, inclusion, and cultural competence to empower individuals from diverse backgrounds to contribute their unique perspectives and talents.

3. Promoting Social Impact and Change:
  - Advocating for Change: Championing social justice, equity, and inclusivity initiatives that empower marginalized or underrepresented groups to advocate for their rights and create systemic change.
  - Community Engagement: Engaging in community service, volunteering, or philanthropy to address local needs, promote civic engagement, and strengthen community bonds.

By actively encouraging and uplifting others, fostering a culture of empowerment, and recognizing the ripple effect of positive actions and contributions, individuals can inspire transformative change, promote collective success, and create a supportive environment where everyone can thrive. This chapter provides practical strategies and insights for empowering others, fostering leadership, and nurturing a culture of encouragement, growth, and empowerment in personal, professional, and community settings.

Chapter 49: Continual Learning

The Wisdom of Discernment
Navigating Life's Good and Bad

The Importance of Lifelong Learning

Lifelong learning is a dynamic and ongoing process of acquiring knowledge, skills, and insights throughout one's life to adapt to change, foster personal growth, and achieve professional success.

1. Adapting to Change and Innovation:
  - Embracing Evolution: Recognizing the rapid pace of technological advancements, industry trends, and societal changes that necessitate continuous learning and skill development.
  - Future-proofing Skills: Proactively updating and expanding knowledge, competencies, and capabilities to remain relevant, adaptable, and competitive in a dynamic global economy.

2. Professional and Personal Growth:
  - Career Advancement: Pursuing professional development opportunities, certifications, or training programs to enhance job performance, expand career opportunities, and achieve career aspirations.
  - Personal Enrichment: Engaging in lifelong learning activities, hobbies, or interests that promote intellectual curiosity, creativity, and personal fulfillment.

Staying Curious and Open-minded

Staying curious and open-minded fosters a mindset of exploration, discovery, and continuous improvement, enabling individuals to embrace new ideas, perspectives, and opportunities for learning and growth.

1. Exploring Diverse Perspectives:
  - Cultural Awareness: Valuing diversity, multiculturalism, and global perspectives to broaden understanding, empathy, and appreciation for different cultures, beliefs, and experiences.
  - Critical Thinking: Developing critical thinking skills to evaluate information, challenge assumptions, and make informed decisions based on evidence, reasoning, and analysis.

2. Seeking New Experiences and Challenges:

   - Stepping Outside Comfort Zones: Embracing challenges, uncertainties, and opportunities that stimulate personal growth, resilience, and adaptability.

   - Experimentation and Innovation: Promoting creativity, innovation, and experimentation to explore new ideas, solutions, and approaches that drive progress and innovation in various domains.

3. Collaboration and Knowledge Sharing:

   - Networking and Collaboration: Collaborating with diverse individuals, teams, and communities to exchange knowledge, share insights, and leverage collective expertise and experiences.

   - Mentorship and Coaching: Engaging in mentorship relationships or coaching partnerships to gain guidance, support, and mentorship from experienced professionals or mentors in respective fields.

By embracing the importance of lifelong learning, staying curious, and fostering an open-minded approach to personal and professional development, individuals can cultivate resilience, adaptability, and a continuous pursuit of excellence in navigating challenges, seizing opportunities, and achieving personal and collective success. This chapter provides practical strategies and insights for integrating lifelong learning into daily routines, fostering a growth mindset, and leveraging learning opportunities to foster personal and professional growth and enrichment.

Chapter 50: The Role of Education

Formal and Informal Learning

Education, in its many forms, is a cornerstone of personal and societal development. Both formal and informal learning experiences contribute to our overall growth and understanding of the world.

1. Formal Education:

- Structured Learning: Formal education involves a structured curriculum, typically delivered in schools, colleges, and universities. It follows a specific path and set of standards aimed at providing comprehensive knowledge and skills in various subjects.

- Qualifications and Credentials: Formal education often leads to qualifications such as diplomas, degrees, and certificates that can enhance career prospects and provide a foundation for further learning.

2. Informal Education:

- Self-Directed Learning: Informal education includes self-directed learning activities outside traditional classroom settings. This can involve reading books, watching educational videos, participating in online courses, and engaging in hobbies.

- Experiential Learning: Learning through life experiences, such as travel, work, and personal projects, also falls under informal education. These experiences can provide practical skills and insights that formal education might not cover.

Lifelong Educational Pursuits

Embracing a lifelong learning mindset is crucial in today's fast-paced, ever-changing world. Continual learning helps individuals stay relevant, adapt to new challenges, and pursue personal growth.

1. Continuous Skill Development:

- Professional Growth: Continuously updating and acquiring new skills is essential for career advancement and staying competitive in the job market. This might include learning new technologies, improving soft skills, or gaining new qualifications.

- Personal Enrichment: Lifelong learning isn't limited to professional development. Pursuing interests and hobbies, learning new languages, or studying new subjects can enrich your personal life and expand your horizons.

2. Staying Curious and Adaptable:

- Curiosity as a Driver: A natural curiosity and desire to learn can drive continuous educational pursuits. Cultivating a curious mindset encourages exploration and discovery in various areas of interest.

The Wisdom of Discernment
Navigating Life's Good and Bad

- Adapting to Change: The ability to learn and adapt quickly is crucial in a world where industries, technologies, and societal norms are constantly evolving. Lifelong learning helps individuals stay agile and responsive to change.

By recognizing the importance of both formal and informal education and committing to lifelong learning, individuals can enhance their personal and professional lives. This chapter explores the various dimensions of education, emphasizing the value of continually expanding one's knowledge and skills throughout life.

Chapter 51: Cultural Intelligence

Understanding Cultural Differences

Cultural intelligence (CQ) is the ability to understand, respect, and effectively interact with people from different cultures. Developing CQ involves recognizing and appreciating the diverse ways in which cultures shape behaviors, values, and communication styles.

1. Recognizing Cultural Norms and Values:
   - Cultural Frameworks: Learn about different cultural frameworks such as Hofstede's cultural dimensions theory, which outlines key differences in values and behaviors across cultures.
   - Cultural Expressions: Understand various cultural expressions, including language, traditions, rituals, and social norms, and how they influence interactions.

2. Avoiding Stereotypes and Biases:
   - Overcoming Preconceptions: Recognize and challenge stereotypes and biases that can lead to misunderstandings and conflicts. Approach each person as an individual rather than a representative of a cultural group.
   - Cultural Relativism: Adopt a culturally relativistic perspective, understanding that different cultures have different ways of seeing the world, and there is no single "right" way.

Navigating Multicultural Interactions

The Wisdom of Discernment
Navigating Life's Good and Bad

Effectively navigating multicultural interactions requires a combination of empathy, communication skills, and adaptability. Building cultural intelligence enhances your ability to work and connect with people from diverse backgrounds.

1. Effective Communication:

  - Verbal and Non-Verbal Communication: Learn to recognize and appropriately respond to both verbal and non-verbal cues that may differ significantly across cultures. Pay attention to body language, eye contact, and gestures.

  - Language Skills: While it's not always necessary to speak the language of every culture you interact with, learning key phrases and demonstrating an effort to communicate can build rapport and show respect.

2. Building Relationships:

  - Trust and Respect: Building trust and mutual respect is crucial in multicultural interactions. Show genuine interest in and respect for cultural differences to foster strong, positive relationships.

  - Collaboration and Teamwork: In professional settings, leverage cultural diversity to enhance creativity, problem-solving, and innovation. Encourage an inclusive environment where all cultural perspectives are valued and considered.

3. Adapting to Different Contexts:

  - Flexibility and Open-Mindedness: Be open to adapting your behavior and communication style to suit different cultural contexts. Flexibility shows respect and a willingness to learn from others.

  - Conflict Resolution: Develop strategies for resolving conflicts that arise from cultural misunderstandings. Approach conflicts with empathy, seeking to understand the cultural context behind differing viewpoints.

By developing cultural intelligence, individuals can enhance their ability to interact effectively in diverse environments, both personally and professionally. This chapter explores the importance of understanding cultural differences and provides practical strategies for navigating multicultural interactions with empathy and respect.

Chapter 52: Developing Resilience

Building Mental Toughness

Resilience is the ability to withstand, adapt to, and recover from adversity and stress. Building mental toughness is a critical component of resilience, enabling individuals to face challenges head-on and maintain a positive outlook.

1. Understanding Mental Toughness:
   - Components of Mental Toughness: Mental toughness encompasses confidence, focus, emotional control, and perseverance. Understanding these components can help you develop strategies to enhance them.
   - Growth Mindset: Adopting a growth mindset, which emphasizes learning and development over fixed abilities, is essential for building mental toughness. Embrace challenges as opportunities for growth rather than obstacles.

2. Techniques for Building Mental Toughness:
   - Self-Discipline: Cultivate self-discipline by setting and adhering to personal goals, maintaining healthy habits, and staying committed to your responsibilities.
   - Positive Thinking: Practice positive thinking by reframing negative thoughts and focusing on solutions rather than problems. Affirmations and visualization can also strengthen your mental fortitude.
   - Stress Management: Learn and implement stress management techniques such as mindfulness, meditation, and deep-breathing exercises to maintain calm and focus under pressure.

Overcoming Adversity

Resilience is often built and tested during times of adversity. Overcoming challenges requires a combination of mental toughness, strategic thinking, and support systems.

1. Facing Challenges Head-On:

The Wisdom of Discernment
Navigating Life's Good and Bad

- Acceptance and Adaptation: Accept the reality of the situation and adapt your strategies to navigate through it. Avoiding or denying challenges can lead to prolonged stress and hinder resilience.

- Problem-Solving Skills: Develop strong problem-solving skills to identify, analyze, and address challenges effectively. Break down problems into manageable parts and tackle them systematically.

2. Building a Support Network:

- Seeking Help and Guidance: Don't hesitate to seek help from friends, family, mentors, or professionals. A strong support network can provide emotional support, practical advice, and different perspectives.

- Community and Connection: Engage with communities and networks that offer support, encouragement, and resources. Being part of a supportive community can enhance your resilience and provide a sense of belonging.

3. Learning from Setbacks:

- Reflection and Growth: Reflect on setbacks to understand what went wrong and what can be learned from the experience. Use these insights to improve and strengthen your approach to future challenges.

- Persistence and Perseverance: Cultivate persistence by staying committed to your goals despite setbacks. Perseverance is key to overcoming adversity and emerging stronger from difficult situations.

By developing resilience, individuals can navigate life's challenges with greater confidence, adaptability, and strength. This chapter explores the importance of building mental toughness and provides practical strategies for overcoming adversity, ensuring that readers are well-equipped to handle whatever life throws their way.

Chapter 53: The Importance of Patience

Practicing Patience in Daily Life

The Wisdom of Discernment

Navigating Life's Good and Bad

Patience is a vital skill that allows individuals to remain calm and composed in the face of delays, obstacles, and frustrations. Practicing patience in daily life can significantly enhance your well-being and interactions with others.

1. Understanding Patience:

   - Definition and Significance: Patience involves the ability to wait calmly for desired outcomes and to endure challenging situations without frustration. It is a cornerstone of emotional intelligence and self-control.

   - Everyday Examples: Patience can be applied in various daily scenarios, such as waiting in traffic, dealing with slow internet connections, or interacting with difficult people.

2. Techniques for Practicing Patience:

   - Mindfulness and Breathing Exercises: Mindfulness practices, such as deep breathing, meditation, and grounding exercises, can help you stay calm and present, reducing impatience.

   - Setting Realistic Expectations: Manage your expectations by setting realistic goals and timelines. Recognize that not everything happens immediately and that progress often takes time.

   - Positive Self-Talk: Use positive self-talk to reinforce patient behavior. Remind yourself that patience leads to better outcomes and helps you maintain control over your reactions.

3. Building a Patience Practice:

   - Daily Reminders: Incorporate reminders into your daily routine to practice patience. This could be a note on your desk, a daily affirmation, or a mindfulness app.

   - Small Steps: Start with small acts of patience in your daily life and gradually work up to more significant challenges. Celebrate your progress to reinforce the habit.

Long-Term Benefits of Being Patient

Patience is not only beneficial in the short term but also offers substantial long-term advantages that can enhance various aspects of your life.

1. Improved Relationships:

- Strengthening Bonds: Patience allows for better communication and understanding in relationships. It helps in resolving conflicts and building stronger, more empathetic connections with others.

- Building Trust: Being patient with others demonstrates respect and consideration, which can build trust and mutual respect over time.

2. Personal Growth and Development:

- Achieving Long-Term Goals: Patience is crucial for pursuing long-term goals and dreams. It helps you stay focused and committed, even when progress is slow.

- Enhanced Resilience: Patience fosters resilience by allowing you to endure setbacks and challenges without becoming discouraged or giving up.

3. Health and Well-Being:

- Reduced Stress and Anxiety: Patience reduces stress and anxiety levels by helping you maintain a calm and composed demeanor in stressful situations.

- Better Decision-Making: Patience leads to more thoughtful and deliberate decision-making, as it allows you to weigh options carefully and avoid impulsive choices.

4. Career and Professional Success:

- Improved Work Performance: Patience enhances your ability to manage workloads, meet deadlines, and collaborate effectively with colleagues, leading to better performance and job satisfaction.

- Leadership Qualities: Patience is a key leadership trait, enabling you to guide and support your team through challenges and changes with a steady hand.

By cultivating patience, you can improve your daily life and enjoy numerous long-term benefits, including stronger relationships, personal growth, better health, and professional success. This chapter provides practical strategies for practicing patience and highlights the enduring positive impact it can have on various aspects of your life.

Chapter 54: Effective Communication

Mastering Verbal and Non-Verbal Communication

The Wisdom of Discernment

Navigating Life's Good and Bad

Effective communication is essential for building strong relationships, achieving personal and professional goals, and understanding others. It involves mastering both verbal and non-verbal communication skills.

1. Verbal Communication:

   - Clarity and Conciseness: Speak clearly and concisely to ensure your message is understood. Avoid using jargon or overly complex language.

   - Tone and Volume: Use an appropriate tone and volume for the situation. A calm and respectful tone can foster positive interactions, while a loud or harsh tone can create tension.

   - Articulation and Pacing: Pay attention to how you articulate words and the pace at which you speak. Speaking too quickly can cause misunderstandings, while speaking too slowly can lose the listener's interest.

2. Non-Verbal Communication:

   - Body Language: Be aware of your body language, including posture, gestures, and facial expressions. Open and relaxed body language can convey approachability and confidence.

   - Eye Contact: Maintain appropriate eye contact to show attentiveness and sincerity. Avoiding eye contact can be perceived as disinterest or dishonesty.

   - Personal Space: Respect personal space to make others feel comfortable. Be mindful of cultural differences regarding personal space and physical contact.

Listening and Understanding

Effective communication is not just about expressing yourself but also about listening to and understanding others. Active listening is a crucial skill that fosters better connections and mutual understanding.

1. Active Listening:

   - Focus and Attention: Give your full attention to the speaker. Avoid distractions and show that you are engaged by nodding, making eye contact, and using verbal acknowledgments like "I see" or "I understand."

- Reflective Listening: Reflect back what the speaker has said to show that you understand. Use phrases like "So what you're saying is..." or "I hear that you are feeling..."

- Avoid Interruptions: Allow the speaker to finish their thoughts without interrupting. This shows respect and ensures you fully understand their message before responding.

2. Empathetic Understanding:

- Put Yourself in Their Shoes: Try to understand the speaker's perspective and emotions. Empathy helps build trust and rapport.

- Responding Appropriately: Respond in a way that acknowledges the speaker's feelings and concerns. Use supportive and validating language to show that you care about their experience.

3. Clarification and Feedback:

- Ask Questions: Ask clarifying questions if you are unsure about something the speaker has said. This ensures accurate understanding and shows that you are engaged in the conversation.

- Provide Constructive Feedback: When giving feedback, be constructive and specific. Focus on behaviors rather than personal attributes and offer solutions or suggestions for improvement.

4. Non-Judgmental Attitude:

- Stay Open-Minded: Approach conversations with an open mind and avoid making snap judgments. Be willing to consider different viewpoints and perspectives.

- Encourage Open Dialogue: Create a safe and supportive environment for open dialogue. Encourage others to share their thoughts and feelings without fear of judgment or criticism.

By mastering verbal and non-verbal communication skills and practicing active listening and empathetic understanding, you can enhance your ability to connect with others, resolve conflicts, and build meaningful relationships. This chapter provides practical strategies for effective communication, emphasizing the importance of both expressing yourself clearly and understanding others deeply.

Chapter 55: Time Management

The Wisdom of Discernment
Navigating Life's Good and Bad

Prioritizing Tasks and Goals

Effective time management is essential for achieving personal and professional success. It involves setting clear priorities and organizing tasks to maximize productivity and minimize stress.

1. Setting Priorities:
   - Identify Key Goals: Start by identifying your key short-term and long-term goals. Understanding what you want to achieve helps you focus your efforts on the most important tasks.
   - Urgent vs. Important: Use the Eisenhower Matrix to categorize tasks based on their urgency and importance. Focus on tasks that are both urgent and important, and schedule or delegate those that are less critical.
   - SMART Goals: Set SMART (Specific, Measurable, Achievable, Relevant, Time-bound) goals to create clear and actionable objectives. This helps you stay focused and track your progress.

2. Task Organization:
   - To-Do Lists: Create daily or weekly to-do lists to keep track of tasks. Break down larger projects into smaller, manageable steps to avoid feeling overwhelmed.
   - Prioritization Techniques: Use techniques like the ABCDE method (assigning A, B, C, D, and E priorities to tasks) or the 1-3-5 rule (one big task, three medium tasks, and five small tasks per day) to organize your workload.

Strategies for Efficient Time Use

Implementing effective time management strategies helps you make the most of your time, increase productivity, and maintain a healthy work-life balance.

1. Planning and Scheduling:
   - Time Blocking: Allocate specific blocks of time for different tasks or activities. This helps you focus on one task at a time and reduces the temptation to multitask.

The Wisdom of Discernment
Navigating Life's Good and Bad

- Daily and Weekly Planning: Plan your day and week in advance, setting aside time for high-priority tasks, meetings, and personal activities. Regularly review and adjust your schedule as needed.

2. Avoiding Procrastination:

- Break Tasks into Steps: Breaking tasks into smaller, manageable steps can make them seem less daunting and help you start working on them sooner.

- Set Deadlines: Establish clear deadlines for tasks, even if they are self-imposed. Having a sense of urgency can motivate you to start and complete tasks on time.

- Use the Pomodoro Technique: Work in focused intervals (typically 25 minutes) followed by short breaks. This can help maintain concentration and prevent burnout.

3. Eliminating Distractions:

- Create a Productive Environment: Set up a workspace that minimizes distractions. Keep your area organized and free from clutter, and use tools like noise-canceling headphones if necessary.

- Limit Digital Distractions: Manage your digital environment by turning off non-essential notifications, using website blockers, and scheduling specific times to check emails and social media.

4. Delegation and Outsourcing:

- Delegate Tasks: Delegate tasks to others when possible, especially those that are less critical or that others can handle more efficiently. This frees up your time for high-priority activities.

- Outsource When Necessary: Consider outsourcing tasks that require specialized skills or that consume a lot of time. This can include hiring freelancers, using virtual assistants, or leveraging automation tools.

5. Maintaining Work-Life Balance:

- Set Boundaries: Establish clear boundaries between work and personal time. Avoid working during designated personal time, and communicate these boundaries to others.

- Schedule Downtime: Make time for relaxation and self-care. Regular breaks and leisure activities are essential for maintaining overall well-being and preventing burnout.

By prioritizing tasks and goals, organizing your workload, and implementing effective time management strategies, you can enhance your productivity, achieve your objectives, and maintain a healthy work-life balance. This chapter provides practical tips and techniques for efficient time use, helping you make the most of each day.

Chapter 56: Stress Management

Techniques to Reduce Stress

Managing stress is crucial for maintaining physical and mental well-being. Various techniques can help reduce stress and promote relaxation.

1. Mindfulness and Meditation:
  - Mindfulness Practices: Engage in mindfulness exercises such as focused breathing, body scans, and mindful observation to stay present and reduce stress.
  - Meditation: Practice meditation regularly to calm the mind and reduce anxiety. Techniques such as guided meditation, transcendental meditation, and loving-kindness meditation can be effective.

2. Physical Activity:
  - Exercise: Regular physical activity, such as walking, running, yoga, or strength training, can help release tension and improve mood. Aim for at least 30 minutes of moderate exercise most days of the week.
  - Stretching and Relaxation Exercises: Incorporate stretching, deep breathing exercises, and progressive muscle relaxation to alleviate physical tension and promote relaxation.

3. Healthy Lifestyle Choices:
  - Balanced Diet: Eat a well-balanced diet rich in fruits, vegetables, lean proteins, and whole grains. Avoid excessive caffeine, sugar, and processed foods that can contribute to stress.
  - Adequate Sleep: Ensure you get enough quality sleep each night. Establish a regular sleep routine and create a restful environment to support restorative sleep.

4. Time Management:

- Organize Tasks: Break down tasks into manageable steps and prioritize them to avoid feeling overwhelmed. Use tools like to-do lists, planners, and time-blocking techniques to stay organized.

- Set Realistic Goals: Set achievable goals and avoid overcommitting yourself. Learn to say no when necessary to prevent burnout.

5. Relaxation Techniques:

- Deep Breathing: Practice deep breathing exercises to reduce immediate stress. Techniques like diaphragmatic breathing can help calm the nervous system.

- Visualization: Use visualization techniques to imagine a peaceful scene or successful outcome. This can help shift your focus away from stressors.

6. Social Support:

- Connect with Others: Spend time with friends and family to share experiences and receive emotional support. Engaging in social activities can provide a sense of belonging and reduce stress.

- Seek Professional Help: If stress becomes overwhelming, consider seeking help from a mental health professional. Therapy, counseling, or support groups can provide valuable coping strategies.

Maintaining Balance in High-Pressure Situations

In high-pressure situations, maintaining balance is essential to manage stress effectively and perform at your best.

1. Preparation and Planning:

- Anticipate Challenges: Identify potential stressors and prepare for them in advance. Having a plan in place can reduce uncertainty and increase confidence.

- Set Priorities: Focus on high-priority tasks and allocate time for essential activities. Avoid multitasking, as it can increase stress and decrease productivity.

2. Staying Calm and Focused:

- Grounding Techniques: Use grounding techniques, such as focusing on your breath or engaging in a sensory activity, to stay present and centered during stressful moments.
- Positive Self-Talk: Replace negative thoughts with positive affirmations and constructive self-talk. Remind yourself of your capabilities and past successes.

3. Taking Breaks:
- Regular Intervals: Schedule regular breaks to rest and recharge. Short breaks can help prevent burnout and maintain overall productivity.
- Change of Scenery: Step away from your workspace and engage in a different activity or environment to refresh your mind.

4. Maintaining Perspective:
- Big Picture Thinking: Keep the bigger picture in mind to avoid getting bogged down by minor stressors. Remind yourself of your long-term goals and values.
- Acceptance and Adaptability: Accept that not everything will go as planned. Adaptability and flexibility can help you navigate unexpected challenges with less stress.

5. Self-Care Practices:
- Nurturing Activities: Engage in activities that bring you joy and relaxation, such as hobbies, reading, or spending time in nature. Prioritize self-care to maintain balance.
- Mind-Body Practices: Incorporate practices like yoga, tai chi, or qigong to connect your mind and body and promote relaxation.

By implementing these stress management techniques and maintaining balance in high-pressure situations, you can reduce stress, enhance well-being, and improve overall performance. This chapter provides practical strategies to help you navigate stress effectively and maintain a healthy, balanced life.

Chapter 57: Goal Setting

Defining Clear Objectives

The Wisdom of Discernment
Navigating Life's Good and Bad

Setting clear and achievable goals is essential for personal and professional growth. Well-defined goals provide direction, motivation, and a sense of purpose.

1. Understanding the Importance of Goals:
  - Purpose and Direction: Goals give you a clear sense of direction and purpose, helping you stay focused on what truly matters.
   - Motivation and Commitment: Having specific goals enhances your motivation and commitment, making it easier to persevere through challenges.

2. Types of Goals:
  - Short-Term Goals: These are goals you aim to achieve in the near future, typically within a few days to a few months. They are often stepping stones to long-term goals.
   - Long-Term Goals: These goals span a longer period, usually several months to years. They require sustained effort and planning.
   - Personal vs. Professional Goals: Personal goals focus on self-improvement and personal fulfillment, while professional goals relate to career advancement and job performance.

3. SMART Goals:
  - Specific: Clearly define what you want to achieve. Avoid vague or broad goals.
  - Measurable: Ensure your goals can be quantified or measured in some way, allowing you to track progress.
   - Achievable: Set realistic goals that are attainable given your current resources and constraints.
  - Relevant: Choose goals that are meaningful and align with your broader objectives.
   - Time-Bound: Set a deadline for achieving your goals to create a sense of urgency and focus.

4. Writing Effective Goals:
  - Clarity and Precision: Write your goals with clear and precise language. Avoid ambiguity.
  - Positive Framing: Frame your goals positively, focusing on what you want to achieve rather than what you want to avoid.

Strategies to Achieve Your Goals

The Wisdom of Discernment
Navigating Life's Good and Bad

Achieving your goals requires a strategic approach, combining planning, action, and continuous evaluation.

1. Planning and Preparation:
   - Break Down Goals: Divide larger goals into smaller, manageable tasks. This makes them less overwhelming and easier to tackle.
   - Create an Action Plan: Develop a detailed action plan outlining the steps you need to take to achieve each goal. Include deadlines and milestones to track progress.

2. Time Management:
   - Prioritize Tasks: Identify the most critical tasks that will have the greatest impact on achieving your goals. Focus on these tasks first.
   - Schedule Time: Allocate specific time blocks in your calendar for working on your goals. Consistent effort over time leads to progress.

3. Overcoming Obstacles:
   - Identify Potential Challenges: Anticipate potential obstacles and plan how to address them. Having contingency plans in place can help you stay on track.
   - Stay Flexible: Be willing to adjust your plans as needed. Flexibility allows you to adapt to changing circumstances without losing sight of your goals.

4. Staying Motivated:
   - Visualize Success: Regularly visualize achieving your goals. This can enhance motivation and reinforce your commitment.
   - Reward Yourself: Celebrate small victories along the way. Recognizing your progress can boost morale and keep you motivated.

5. Accountability and Support:
   - Share Your Goals: Tell someone you trust about your goals. This adds a layer of accountability and can provide encouragement and support.
   - Seek Feedback: Regularly seek feedback from others to gain new perspectives and improve your approach.

6. Continuous Evaluation and Adjustment:
   - Monitor Progress: Regularly review your progress towards your goals. Track your achievements and identify areas where you may need to adjust your strategy.
  - Reflect and Adjust: Reflect on what is working and what is not. Make necessary adjustments to your action plan and stay committed to your objectives.

7. Mindset and Resilience:
  - Stay Positive: Maintain a positive mindset, even when facing setbacks. Resilience is key to overcoming challenges and continuing your pursuit of goals.
   - Learn from Failures: View failures as learning opportunities. Analyze what went wrong, make improvements, and keep moving forward.

By defining clear objectives and implementing effective strategies, you can set and achieve meaningful goals that contribute to your personal and professional growth. This chapter provides practical tips and techniques to help you navigate the goal-setting process and turn your aspirations into reality.

Chapter 58: Building Self-Confidence

Understanding Self-Worth

Self-confidence stems from a strong sense of self-worth. Understanding and valuing yourself is the foundation for building lasting confidence.

1. Defining Self-Worth:
   - Intrinsic Value: Recognize that your worth is inherent and not based on external achievements or validation. Everyone has intrinsic value just by being themselves.
   - Self-Respect: Treat yourself with respect and kindness. Acknowledge your strengths and accept your imperfections.

2. Self-Perception:

- Positive Self-Image: Cultivate a positive self-image by focusing on your strengths and accomplishments rather than dwelling on perceived flaws or failures.

- Self-Compassion: Practice self-compassion by being gentle with yourself during times of struggle. Understand that everyone experiences setbacks and it's part of the human experience.

3. Challenging Negative Beliefs:

- Identify Negative Thoughts: Recognize and challenge negative beliefs about yourself. Replace them with positive affirmations and realistic assessments of your abilities.

- Cognitive Restructuring: Use cognitive restructuring techniques to reframe negative thoughts and develop a more balanced and positive mindset.

4. Accepting Yourself:

- Self-Acceptance: Embrace all aspects of yourself, including your strengths and weaknesses. Accepting yourself as you are is crucial for building genuine self-confidence.

- Authenticity: Be true to yourself and your values. Authenticity fosters a sense of integrity and self-worth.

Techniques to Boost Confidence

Building self-confidence involves both internal and external strategies that reinforce your belief in yourself and your abilities.

1. Setting and Achieving Goals:

- Small Wins: Set achievable short-term goals and celebrate each accomplishment. Small wins build momentum and reinforce your confidence.

- Incremental Challenges: Gradually take on more challenging tasks to stretch your abilities and build confidence through experience.

2. Skill Development:

- Continuous Learning: Engage in continuous learning and self-improvement. Developing new skills and knowledge boosts your competence and confidence.

- Practice and Preparation: Practice regularly to hone your skills. Adequate preparation reduces anxiety and increases your confidence in your abilities.

3. Positive Affirmations:
  - Daily Affirmations: Incorporate positive affirmations into your daily routine. Affirmations like "I am capable," "I am confident," and "I believe in myself" can reinforce a positive self-concept.
  - Visualization: Visualize yourself succeeding in various scenarios. Visualization helps create a mental image of success, enhancing your confidence in real-life situations.

4. Body Language and Posture:
  - Confident Posture: Maintain an upright posture, make eye contact, and use open body language. Confident body language can positively influence your mindset and how others perceive you.
  - Power Poses: Practice power poses, such as standing with your hands on your hips, to boost feelings of confidence and reduce stress.

5. Facing Fears:
  - Gradual Exposure: Gradually expose yourself to situations that make you anxious. Facing your fears incrementally can desensitize you to anxiety triggers and build confidence.
  - Reframing Fear: Reframe fear as a natural part of growth. View challenges as opportunities to learn and improve, rather than as threats.

6. Seeking Feedback and Support:
  - Constructive Feedback: Seek constructive feedback from trusted individuals to gain insights into your strengths and areas for improvement. Use feedback to grow and enhance your confidence.
  - Supportive Relationships: Surround yourself with supportive and positive people who encourage and believe in you. Supportive relationships reinforce your self-worth and confidence.

7. Self-Care and Well-Being:

The Wisdom of Discernment
Navigating Life's Good and Bad

- Healthy Lifestyle: Maintain a healthy lifestyle through regular exercise, balanced nutrition, and adequate sleep. Physical well-being contributes to mental and emotional confidence.
- Stress Management: Use stress management techniques, such as mindfulness, meditation, and relaxation exercises, to stay calm and focused.

8. Embracing Failure as a Learning Tool:
- Learning from Mistakes: View failures as valuable learning experiences. Analyze what went wrong, make adjustments, and apply the lessons to future endeavors.
- Resilience Building: Develop resilience by bouncing back from setbacks. Each recovery strengthens your confidence in handling future challenges.

By understanding self-worth and employing techniques to boost confidence, you can develop a strong, resilient sense of self. This chapter provides practical strategies to help you build and maintain self-confidence, empowering you to pursue your goals and navigate life with assurance and poise.

Chapter 59: Understanding Motivation

Intrinsic and Extrinsic Motivation

Motivation drives our behavior and influences our actions toward achieving goals. Understanding the different types of motivation can help you harness it effectively.

1. Intrinsic Motivation:
- Internal Drive: Intrinsic motivation comes from within and is driven by personal satisfaction, enjoyment, or a sense of purpose.
- Examples: Pursuing activities because they are inherently rewarding, such as hobbies, personal interests, or creative endeavors.
- Benefits: Intrinsic motivation fosters engagement, creativity, and long-term satisfaction. It aligns with personal values and interests, leading to sustained effort and perseverance.

2. Extrinsic Motivation:

- External Rewards: Extrinsic motivation involves seeking rewards or avoiding punishment from external sources, such as recognition, praise, money, or grades.

- Examples: Working towards a promotion at work, studying for grades, or completing tasks for bonuses or incentives.

- Benefits and Challenges: Extrinsic motivation can provide short-term boosts in productivity and effort. However, reliance solely on external rewards may undermine intrinsic motivation and lead to burnout if rewards are not consistently provided.

3. Balancing Intrinsic and Extrinsic Motivation:

- Complementary Roles: Both types of motivation can complement each other in achieving goals. Combining intrinsic satisfaction with extrinsic rewards can enhance motivation and sustain long-term commitment.

- Alignment with Goals: Aligning tasks with personal values and interests (intrinsic) while recognizing achievements and rewards (extrinsic) creates a balanced motivational approach.

Staying Motivated Over Time

Maintaining motivation over the long term requires strategies that sustain enthusiasm, manage setbacks, and foster continuous progress.

1. Setting Meaningful Goals:

- Purpose and Clarity: Define clear, meaningful goals that align with your values and aspirations. Establishing a sense of purpose enhances intrinsic motivation and commitment.

- SMART Goals: Use SMART criteria (Specific, Measurable, Achievable, Relevant, Time-bound) to structure goals effectively and track progress.

2. Finding Purpose and Passion:

- Connecting to Values: Identify tasks or activities that resonate with your core values and interests. Passion fuels intrinsic motivation and drives sustained effort.

- Personal Growth: Seek opportunities for personal growth and development that inspire and challenge you. Continuously expanding skills and knowledge sustains motivation.

3. Celebrating Milestones:

- Acknowledging Achievements: Celebrate small wins and milestones along the way. Acknowledging progress reinforces motivation and builds momentum toward larger goals.

- Reward Systems: Establish personal reward systems for reaching milestones or completing tasks. Rewards can be intrinsic (personal satisfaction) or extrinsic (tangible rewards).

4. Managing Challenges and Setbacks:

- Resilience Building: Cultivate resilience to navigate obstacles and setbacks effectively. View challenges as opportunities for learning and growth rather than deterrents.

- Problem-Solving Skills: Develop problem-solving skills to address barriers and find alternative solutions. Adaptability enhances motivation by reducing frustration and uncertainty.

5. Creating a Supportive Environment:

- Social Support: Surround yourself with supportive individuals who encourage and motivate you. Collaborate with peers, mentors, or coaches who provide guidance and feedback.

- Accountability Partners: Partner with accountability buddies or mentors to stay accountable and motivated. Regular check-ins and mutual support foster commitment and progress.

6. Maintaining Well-being and Balance:

- Self-Care: Prioritize self-care practices, such as adequate sleep, exercise, and relaxation techniques. Physical and mental well-being sustains energy levels and resilience.

- Work-Life Balance: Establish boundaries and allocate time for activities that recharge and rejuvenate you. Balance prevents burnout and supports sustained motivation.

7. Continuous Learning and Adaptation:

- Learning Mindset: Embrace a growth mindset that values continuous learning and improvement. Embrace challenges as opportunities to expand skills and knowledge.

- Feedback and Reflection: Seek feedback to gain insights into your progress and areas for development. Reflect on experiences to refine goals and strategies over time.

Understanding motivation involves recognizing the interplay between intrinsic and extrinsic factors while implementing strategies to sustain enthusiasm and progress. By aligning goals with personal values, celebrating achievements, managing setbacks effectively, and cultivating a supportive environment, you can foster enduring motivation to pursue your aspirations and thrive in various aspects of life.

Chapter 60: Practicing Gratitude

The Benefits of a Grateful Attitude

Gratitude is a powerful emotion that enhances overall well-being and enriches personal relationships. Cultivating a grateful attitude brings numerous benefits to your life.

1. Emotional Well-being:
  - Positive Emotions: Gratitude promotes positive feelings such as happiness, contentment, and satisfaction. It shifts focus from what is lacking to what is present and appreciated.
    - Resilience: Grateful individuals tend to cope better with stress and adversity. Acknowledging blessings fosters resilience by reframing challenges in a more positive light.

2. Improved Relationships:
  - Enhanced Connections: Expressing gratitude strengthens relationships by fostering trust, empathy, and mutual appreciation. It reinforces bonds and encourages supportive behaviors.
    - Generosity: Grateful individuals are more likely to engage in acts of kindness and generosity towards others. Gratitude creates a ripple effect of positivity within social networks.

3. Physical Health Benefits:
  - Stress Reduction: Gratitude reduces stress hormones and promotes relaxation, which contributes to better cardiovascular health and immune function.
  - Quality of Sleep: Grateful individuals often experience improved sleep quality, leading to greater overall health and vitality.

4. Psychological Benefits:

   - Mindfulness and Presence: Practicing gratitude cultivates mindfulness by focusing attention on the present moment and appreciating simple pleasures.

   - Self-esteem: Grateful individuals tend to have higher self-esteem and a more positive self-image. Acknowledging blessings reinforces a sense of personal worth and accomplishment.

Daily Gratitude Practices

Incorporating daily gratitude practices into your routine can amplify the benefits of a grateful attitude, fostering a more optimistic outlook and enhancing overall happiness.

1. Gratitude Journaling:

   - Reflective Writing: Dedicate time each day to write down things you are grateful for. This practice encourages self-reflection and mindfulness.

   - Specificity: Be specific about what you appreciate and why. Focus on both big and small blessings in your life.

2. Expressing Gratitude to Others:

   - Verbal Appreciation: Express gratitude directly to others through sincere compliments, thank-you notes, or verbal acknowledgments. Genuine appreciation strengthens relationships.

   - Acts of Kindness: Show gratitude through acts of kindness and support. Actions speak louder than words and contribute to a positive, supportive environment.

3. Gratitude Rituals:

   - Morning Reflection: Start your day by reflecting on three things you are grateful for. This sets a positive tone and mindset for the day ahead.

   - Evening Gratitude: Before bed, recall moments or experiences from the day that brought you joy or gratitude. End the day on a positive note.

4. Gratitude Meditation:

The Wisdom of Discernment
Navigating Life's Good and Bad

- Mindful Practice: Incorporate gratitude into mindfulness or meditation sessions. Focus on feelings of gratitude and appreciation, allowing them to permeate your thoughts and emotions.
- Visual Imagery: Visualize scenes or memories that evoke feelings of gratitude. Imagine yourself surrounded by warmth and positivity.

5. Gratitude Challenges or Projects:
- Weekly or Monthly Challenges: Participate in gratitude challenges where you commit to finding and acknowledging specific blessings each day for a set period.
- Gratitude Boards or Journals: Create visual reminders of gratitude by compiling photos, quotes, or memories that evoke feelings of appreciation.

6. Gratitude in Adversity:
- Finding Silver Linings: During difficult times, intentionally seek out silver linings or lessons learned. Practicing gratitude in adversity enhances resilience and perspective.
- Perspective Shift: Reframe challenges as opportunities for growth or moments of clarity. Acknowledge strengths and resources that support you through tough times.

By embracing gratitude as a daily practice, you can nurture a positive mindset, strengthen relationships, and enhance your overall well-being. The benefits of cultivating gratitude extend beyond personal happiness to encompass resilience, empathy, and a deeper appreciation for life's joys and challenges alike.

Chapter 61: Self-Discipline

Developing Willpower

Self-discipline is the ability to control one's impulses, emotions, and behaviors in order to achieve goals. Developing strong willpower is essential for personal growth and achieving long-term success.

1. Understanding Willpower:

The Wisdom of Discernment

Navigating Life's Good and Bad

- Definition: Willpower is the mental strength to resist short-term temptations or distractions in favor of long-term goals.

- Self-Control: It involves managing impulses, emotions, and actions in alignment with your values and objectives.

2. Building Self-Discipline:

- Setting Clear Goals: Define specific, measurable goals that align with your values and aspirations. Clear objectives provide direction and motivation.

- Creating Habits: Establish routines and habits that support your goals. Consistent actions build momentum and reinforce self-discipline over time.

3. Strategies for Strengthening Willpower:

- Delaying Gratification: Practice delaying immediate rewards for greater long-term benefits. Develop patience and resilience in pursuing your goals.

- Resisting Temptations: Identify triggers or temptations that undermine your progress. Use strategies like distraction, substitution, or avoidance to maintain focus.

4. Mindfulness and Self-Awareness:

- Awareness of Triggers: Be mindful of situations, emotions, or environments that challenge your self-discipline. Self-awareness enhances your ability to make intentional choices.

- Staying Present: Practice mindfulness techniques to stay present and focused on your goals. Mindful awareness reduces impulsivity and strengthens decision-making.

5. Building Motivation:

- Intrinsic Motivation: Connect goals to personal values and intrinsic motivations. Genuine interest and passion sustain motivation and commitment.

- Reward Systems: Use rewards as incentives for achieving milestones or maintaining disciplined behaviors. Positive reinforcement reinforces self-discipline.

6. Practicing Consistency:

- Daily Commitments: Commit to daily practices that support your goals, even when motivation wanes. Consistency builds habits and reinforces self-discipline as a routine.

- Accountability: Hold yourself accountable to goals and commitments. Seek support from mentors, peers, or accountability partners to stay on track.

Long-Term Benefits of Discipline

Self-discipline yields significant benefits that extend beyond achieving immediate goals, influencing various aspects of life and personal development.

1. Achievement of Goals:
   - Goal Attainment: Discipline enables you to set, pursue, and achieve ambitious goals. Consistent effort and perseverance lead to tangible accomplishments.
   - Personal Growth: Overcoming challenges through self-discipline fosters resilience, confidence, and a sense of achievement.

2. Improved Time Management:
   - Efficiency and Productivity: Discipline enhances time management skills by prioritizing tasks, maintaining focus, and minimizing distractions. Effective use of time maximizes productivity.

3. Enhanced Mental Health:
   - Stress Reduction: Managing impulses and maintaining self-control reduces stress levels. Discipline fosters emotional stability and resilience in coping with challenges.
   - Mental Well-being: Consistent disciplined habits contribute to a sense of purpose, satisfaction, and overall well-being.

4. Positive Relationships:
   - Reliability and Trustworthiness: Demonstrating self-discipline builds trust and reliability in relationships. Consistent behaviors foster respect and strengthen interpersonal connections.
   - Conflict Resolution: Discipline promotes constructive communication and conflict resolution skills, enhancing relationship dynamics.

5. Financial Stability:

- Financial Planning: Discipline in financial habits, such as budgeting and saving, leads to long-term financial security and independence.

- Debt Management: Avoiding impulsive spending and adhering to financial goals supports debt management and wealth accumulation.

6. Health and Wellness:

- Healthy Lifestyle: Discipline contributes to maintaining physical health through regular exercise, balanced nutrition, and adequate rest.

- Preventative Care: Consistent health habits reduce the risk of illness and promote longevity.

By cultivating self-discipline and strengthening willpower, you empower yourself to overcome challenges, achieve personal goals, and lead a fulfilling life. The long-term benefits of discipline extend across personal, professional, and relational domains, fostering resilience, success, and well-being.

Certainly! Here's a structured approach for Chapter 62 on Adaptability in Change:

Chapter 62: Adaptability in Change

Embracing Life's Transitions

Change is a constant in life, and learning to adapt smoothly can greatly enhance our resilience and growth. Embracing life's transitions involves understanding the nature of change and preparing ourselves to navigate through it with grace and effectiveness.

1. Understanding Adaptability:

- Definition: Adaptability is the ability to adjust and respond effectively to new circumstances or unexpected changes.

- Importance: Embracing adaptability allows us to thrive in dynamic environments, fostering personal growth and resilience.

2. Embracing Life's Transitions:

- Mindset Shift: Cultivate a mindset that views change as an opportunity for growth rather than a threat. Embrace uncertainty as a chance to learn and evolve.
- Acceptance: Acknowledge that change is inevitable and a natural part of life. Embracing transitions with acceptance reduces resistance and facilitates smoother adaptation.

3. Strategies for Adapting Smoothly:
- Flexibility: Develop flexibility in thinking and behavior. Be open to different perspectives and approaches to situations.
- Problem-Solving: Enhance problem-solving skills to effectively address challenges that arise during transitions. Break down complex problems into manageable steps.

4. Building Resilience:
- Resilience Practices: Engage in practices that promote resilience, such as mindfulness, self-care, and maintaining a positive outlook.
- Learning from Setbacks: Use setbacks as opportunities for learning and growth. Reflect on experiences to glean insights and strengthen resilience for future transitions.

5. Seeking Support:
- Social Networks: Build a supportive network of friends, family, and mentors who can provide encouragement and guidance during times of change.
- Professional Support: Seek professional guidance or coaching to navigate career transitions or personal challenges effectively.

6. Adapting to Personal Growth:
- Continuous Learning: Foster a mindset of continuous learning and personal development. Acquire new skills and knowledge to adapt to evolving circumstances.
- Self-Reflection: Regularly reflect on personal goals and values. Align actions with aspirations to ensure that transitions contribute to long-term fulfillment.

By embracing adaptability, we empower ourselves to navigate life's transitions with resilience, confidence, and a sense of purpose. Embracing change as an opportunity for growth enables us to thrive in an ever-changing world, fostering personal and professional success.

The Wisdom of Discernment
Navigating Life's Good and Bad

Chapter 63: Finding Balance

Work-Life Balance

Finding balance between personal and professional life is crucial for overall well-being and sustained success. Balancing commitments, responsibilities, and personal growth enhances fulfillment and productivity in both spheres.

1. Understanding Work-Life Balance:
  - Definition: Work-life balance refers to prioritizing and managing commitments between work (career and ambitions) and personal life (family, health, leisure).
  - Importance: Achieving balance ensures holistic well-being, reduces stress, and promotes long-term happiness and productivity.

2. Strategies for Work-Life Balance:
  - Setting Priorities: Identify and prioritize tasks and activities based on importance and urgency. Allocate time and energy accordingly to maintain equilibrium.
  - Time Management: Implement effective time management techniques, such as prioritizing tasks, setting boundaries, and delegating responsibilities when possible.

3. Balancing Personal and Professional Life:
  - Establishing Boundaries: Define clear boundaries between work and personal life. Allocate specific times for work and leisure activities to prevent overlap and burnout.
  - Switching Off: Practice detachment from work during personal time. Disconnect from emails and work-related tasks to recharge and rejuvenate.

4. Promoting Well-being:
  - Self-Care Practices: Prioritize self-care activities, such as exercise, meditation, and hobbies, to maintain physical and mental health.
  - Healthy Lifestyle: Incorporate healthy habits into daily routines, including nutritious eating, adequate sleep, and regular breaks during work hours.

5. Communication and Support:

   - Open Communication: Communicate openly with employers, colleagues, and family members about your availability and needs. Foster understanding and support for your balanced lifestyle.

   - Seeking Assistance: Delegate tasks at work and enlist support from family and friends when needed. Collaboration and mutual assistance promote efficiency and reduce stress.

6. Personal Growth and Development:

   - Continuous Learning: Engage in ongoing personal and professional development. Set goals for growth and achievement in both personal and career domains.

   - Flexibility and Adaptability: Embrace flexibility to adjust plans and priorities as circumstances change. Adaptability fosters resilience and enhances overall balance.

Achieving work-life balance requires conscious effort and commitment to prioritize well-being alongside professional responsibilities. By implementing strategies for effective time management, establishing clear boundaries, promoting self-care, and fostering open communication, individuals can cultivate a harmonious equilibrium that supports long-term success and fulfillment in all aspects of life.

Chapter 64: The Power of Positivity

Cultivating a Positive Mindset

Maintaining a positive mindset can significantly influence one's perspective, behaviors, and overall life outcomes. Cultivating positivity involves adopting constructive thought patterns and fostering optimism in daily life.

1. Understanding Positivity:

   - Definition: Positivity involves maintaining an optimistic outlook, focusing on strengths and opportunities rather than dwelling on negatives.

   - Mindset Shift: Cultivate a mindset that sees challenges as opportunities for growth and learning.

2. Strategies for Cultivating Positivity:

- Gratitude Practices: Regularly practice gratitude by acknowledging and appreciating blessings, both big and small.

- Positive Affirmations: Use positive affirmations to reinforce self-belief and optimism. Repeat affirmations that promote confidence and resilience.

3. Mindfulness and Awareness:

- Present Moment Awareness: Practice mindfulness techniques to stay present and attentive to the current moment. Mindfulness reduces stress and enhances clarity.

- Thought Monitoring: Monitor and challenge negative thoughts. Replace them with positive, empowering thoughts to shift perspective.

4. Building Resilience:

- Adaptability: Embrace change and uncertainty with resilience. View setbacks as temporary challenges rather than permanent obstacles.

- Self-Efficacy: Develop a belief in your ability to overcome challenges and achieve goals. Self-efficacy enhances motivation and perseverance.

5. Promoting Positive Relationships:

- Kindness and Empathy: Practice kindness and empathy in interactions with others. Positive relationships foster a supportive environment and enhance well-being.

- Conflict Resolution: Approach conflicts with a positive attitude and a willingness to find constructive solutions. Effective conflict resolution strengthens relationships.

Impact of Positivity on Life Outcomes

1. Emotional Well-being:

- Enhanced Happiness: Positivity contributes to a greater sense of happiness and fulfillment in life. Optimistic individuals experience more joy and satisfaction.

2. Physical Health:

- Stress Reduction: Maintaining a positive outlook reduces stress levels, which supports cardiovascular health and boosts immune function.

The Wisdom of Discernment

Navigating Life's Good and Bad

- Longevity: Studies suggest that optimistic individuals tend to live longer and healthier lives compared to those with a negative outlook.

3. Professional Success:
   - Productivity: Positivity enhances motivation and productivity at work. Optimistic individuals are more likely to persevere through challenges and achieve career goals.
   - Leadership: Positive leaders inspire and motivate teams, fostering a supportive work environment and driving organizational success.

4. Personal Growth:
   - Resilience: Cultivating a positive mindset builds resilience to cope with setbacks and adversity. Optimism enables individuals to bounce back stronger from challenges.
   - Self-Improvement: Positive individuals are more open to personal development and continuous learning, which facilitates growth and achievement of goals.

5. Social Connections:
   - Attractiveness: Positive individuals tend to attract and maintain positive social connections. Optimism creates a favorable impression and fosters meaningful relationships.
   - Community Impact: Optimistic individuals contribute positively to their communities by spreading kindness, empathy, and inspiration.

By embracing positivity and cultivating a resilient mindset, individuals can enhance their overall well-being, achieve greater success in various aspects of life, and positively impact their surroundings. Emphasizing gratitude, mindfulness, and constructive thought patterns fosters a mindset that promotes happiness, fulfillment, and long-term success.

Chapter 65: Healthy Living

Nutrition and Exercise

Healthy living encompasses practices that promote physical, mental, and emotional well-being. Focusing on nutrition, exercise, and mental health contributes to a balanced and fulfilling lifestyle.

The Wisdom of Discernment
Navigating Life's Good and Bad

1. Nutrition:

   - Balanced Diet: Maintain a balanced diet rich in fruits, vegetables, whole grains, lean proteins, and healthy fats.

   - Hydration: Drink an adequate amount of water daily to support bodily functions and overall health.

   - Portion Control: Practice portion control to manage calorie intake and maintain a healthy weight.

2. Exercise:

   - Regular Physical Activity: Engage in regular exercise that includes cardiovascular activities, strength training, and flexibility exercises.

   - Benefits: Exercise improves cardiovascular health, enhances muscle strength, boosts mood, and reduces stress.

Mental and Emotional Well-being

1. Stress Management:

   - Techniques: Use stress management techniques such as deep breathing, meditation, yoga, or mindfulness to reduce stress levels.

   - Work-Life Balance: Maintain a healthy balance between work, personal life, and leisure activities to prevent burnout.

2. Emotional Health:

   - Self-Care: Prioritize self-care activities that promote relaxation and mental clarity, such as hobbies, reading, or spending time in nature.

   - Seeking Support: Reach out to friends, family, or a therapist for emotional support during challenging times.

Integrating Healthy Practices

1. Holistic Approach:

- Mind-Body Connection: Recognize the interconnectedness of physical, mental, and emotional health. Addressing one aspect positively impacts overall well-being.
- Consistency: Maintain consistency in healthy habits to establish long-term benefits and sustain positive lifestyle changes.

2. Personalized Approach:
  - Individual Needs: Tailor nutrition, exercise, and mental health practices to suit individual preferences and health goals.
  - Continuous Improvement: Strive for continuous improvement in healthy living practices by setting realistic goals and monitoring progress.

By prioritizing nutrition, regular exercise, stress management, and emotional well-being, individuals can cultivate a healthy lifestyle that supports longevity, vitality, and overall happiness. Adopting a holistic approach to health promotes resilience, enhances quality of life, and empowers individuals to achieve their full potential.

Chapter 66: Creating a Vision Board

Visualizing Goals and Dreams

Creating a vision board is a powerful tool for manifesting dreams and goals by visually representing aspirations and fostering focus and motivation.

1. Visualizing Goals:
  - Clarity: Define specific goals and dreams in various areas of life, such as career, relationships, health, and personal growth.
  - Visualization: Imagine achieving these goals in vivid detail, focusing on how it feels and looks to accomplish them.

2. Benefits of Vision Boards:
  - Clarifying Intentions: Articulate and prioritize goals by selecting images, words, and symbols that represent aspirations and values.

The Wisdom of Discernment

Navigating Life's Good and Bad

- Inspiration and Motivation: Stay inspired and motivated by visualizing goals regularly, reinforcing commitment and perseverance.

Using Vision Boards to Stay Focused

1. Creating Your Vision Board:
  - Gather Materials: Collect magazines, photos, quotes, and other visual elements that resonate with your goals.
  - Design Layout: Arrange and affix chosen images and words onto a board or digital platform, organizing them in a meaningful and inspiring way.

2. Visual Representation:
  - Meaningful Imagery: Select images that evoke positive emotions and align with your desired outcomes.
  - Personalization: Customize your vision board to reflect your unique aspirations and values, ensuring it resonates deeply with your goals.

3. Regular Review and Reflection:
  - Routine Check-ins: Set aside time regularly to review your vision board, reinforcing your commitment and tracking progress toward goals.
  - Adjustments and Updates: Modify your vision board as goals evolve or are achieved, maintaining relevance and alignment with your current aspirations.

4. Manifestation and Action:
  - Goal Setting: Break down larger goals into smaller, actionable steps. Use your vision board as a roadmap to guide your actions and decisions.
  - Visualization Techniques: Visualize success and achievement regularly, leveraging your vision board to maintain focus and intention.

Creating and utilizing a vision board is a proactive approach to manifesting dreams and goals, fostering clarity, motivation, and sustained focus. By regularly engaging with your vision board and aligning actions with aspirations, you empower yourself to turn dreams into reality and achieve meaningful personal and professional growth.

The Wisdom of Discernment
Navigating Life's Good and Bad

Chapter 67: The Science of Happiness

Understanding What Makes Us Happy

Exploring the science of happiness unveils key factors and practices that contribute to overall well-being and life satisfaction.

1. Psychological Foundations:
 - Definition: Happiness is a subjective state characterized by positive emotions, satisfaction with life, and a sense of fulfillment.
 - Factors: Identify factors that influence happiness, including genetics, life circumstances, and intentional activities.

2. Key Components of Happiness:
 - Positive Emotions: Cultivate positive emotions such as joy, gratitude, and contentment through daily practices and mindful awareness.
 - Life Satisfaction: Assess and enhance satisfaction with life by focusing on meaningful goals and personal values.

Incorporating Happiness into Daily Life

1. Positive Psychology Practices:
 - Gratitude: Practice gratitude by reflecting on and appreciating positive aspects of daily life, fostering a grateful mindset.
 - Mindfulness: Engage in mindfulness practices to stay present, reduce stress, and enhance overall well-being.

2. Social Connections:
 - Relationships: Cultivate and nurture positive relationships with family, friends, and community members, as social connections are integral to happiness.
 - Support Networks: Build and maintain support networks that provide emotional support and companionship during challenging times.

3. Meaning and Purpose:
  - Personal Growth: Pursue activities and goals that align with personal values and contribute to a sense of purpose and fulfillment.
  - Contribution: Engage in acts of kindness and altruism, as contributing to the well-being of others enhances personal happiness.

4. Health and Well-being:
  - Physical Health: Prioritize physical health through regular exercise, nutritious eating, and adequate sleep, which positively impact mood and overall happiness.
  - Emotional Well-being: Manage stress effectively, seek professional support when needed, and engage in self-care practices that promote mental health.

5. Continuous Learning and Growth:
  - Lifelong Learning: Embrace opportunities for learning and skill development, as acquiring new knowledge and experiences enriches life satisfaction.
  - Adaptability: Cultivate resilience and adaptability to navigate challenges and setbacks with optimism and perseverance.

Understanding the science of happiness empowers individuals to adopt evidence-based practices that enhance well-being and life satisfaction. By integrating happiness-promoting activities into daily routines and prioritizing factors such as positive emotions, meaningful relationships, and personal growth, individuals can cultivate a fulfilling and joyful life.

Chapter 68: Mindful Living

Principles of Mindfulness

Mindfulness is a practice rooted in awareness and presence, fostering a deeper connection with the present moment and enhancing overall well-being.

1. Definition of Mindfulness:

- Present Moment Awareness: Mindfulness involves paying attention to the present moment with openness, curiosity, and acceptance.

- Non-Judgmental Observation: Cultivate a non-judgmental attitude toward thoughts, emotions, and sensations that arise during mindfulness practice.

2. Core Principles of Mindfulness:

- Awareness: Develop heightened awareness of internal experiences (thoughts, emotions, physical sensations) and external surroundings.

- Acceptance: Embrace experiences without resistance or attachment, acknowledging them as transient and part of the human experience.

Incorporating Mindfulness Practices

1. Mindfulness Meditation:

- Techniques: Practice formal meditation techniques, such as focused attention (e.g., on breath or bodily sensations) and open monitoring (e.g., observing thoughts without attachment).

- Benefits: Experience benefits such as stress reduction, improved focus, emotional regulation, and enhanced overall well-being.

2. Daily Mindfulness in Daily Life:

- Routine Practices: Integrate mindfulness into daily routines, such as mindful eating, walking, or commuting.

- Mindful Pause: Take mindful pauses throughout the day to ground yourself in the present moment and reduce stress.

3. Mindful Relationships:

- Presence: Be fully present and attentive during interactions with others, fostering deeper connections and communication.

- Empathy: Cultivate empathy and compassion through mindful listening and understanding of others' perspectives and emotions.

4. Mindful Self-Care:

The Wisdom of Discernment
Navigating Life's Good and Bad

- Self-Compassion: Practice self-compassion by treating yourself with kindness and understanding, especially during challenging times.
- Stress Management: Use mindfulness techniques to manage stress, reduce anxiety, and promote relaxation and mental clarity.

5. Mindful Awareness of Emotions:
- Emotional Regulation: Develop skills for recognizing and regulating emotions through mindfulness, promoting emotional resilience and well-being.
- Response vs. Reaction: Pause and respond consciously to situations rather than reacting impulsively, fostering mindful decision-making.

Benefits of Mindful Living

1. Stress Reduction: Mindfulness reduces stress by promoting relaxation and easing tension in the body and mind.
2. Emotional Well-being: Enhances emotional resilience, self-awareness, and the ability to manage difficult emotions effectively.
3. Cognitive Function: Improves concentration, attention, and cognitive flexibility, leading to better decision-making and problem-solving.
4. Physical Health: Supports physical health through better sleep, immune function, and overall vitality.
5. Relationships: Deepens interpersonal connections by fostering empathy, active listening, and authentic communication.

By embracing the principles of mindfulness and incorporating regular mindfulness practices into daily life, individuals can cultivate greater awareness, resilience, and overall well-being. Mindful living enables a deeper appreciation of the present moment and empowers individuals to respond to life's challenges with clarity, compassion, and inner peace.

Chapter 69: The Power of Habits

Forming Positive Habits

The Wisdom of Discernment
Navigating Life's Good and Bad

Understanding the mechanisms of habit formation and modification empowers individuals to cultivate positive behaviors and break free from negative patterns.

1. Definition of Habits:
   - Routine Behaviors: Habits are automatic, repeated behaviors that are often performed unconsciously in response to cues or triggers.
   - Neurological Basis: Habits are ingrained through neuroplasticity, with repeated actions strengthening neural pathways in the brain.

2. Steps to Forming Positive Habits:
   - Identify Goals: Define specific, achievable goals that align with your values and aspirations.
   - Start Small: Begin with manageable actions that are easy to integrate into your daily routine.
   - Consistency: Repeat the behavior consistently over time to reinforce the habit loop.

Breaking Negative Habits

1. Recognizing Negative Habits:
   - Awareness: Identify behaviors or routines that contribute to negative outcomes or detract from your well-being.
   - Triggers: Recognize triggers or cues that prompt negative habits, such as stress, boredom, or specific environmental cues.

2. Strategies for Breaking Negative Habits:
   - Replace with Positive Alternatives: Substitute negative habits with healthier, more constructive behaviors that serve your goals.
   - Modify Environment: Modify your environment to reduce exposure to triggers or cues that reinforce negative habits.
   - Mindfulness and Self-Reflection: Use mindfulness techniques and self-reflection to become more aware of triggers and responses, fostering conscious decision-making.

3. Support Systems:

The Wisdom of Discernment
Navigating Life's Good and Bad

- Accountability: Seek support from friends, family, or a mentor who can provide encouragement and accountability.

- Professional Help: Consider seeking professional assistance, such as therapy or counseling, to address underlying causes of negative habits.

Benefits of Habit Mastery

1. Efficiency and Productivity: Establishing positive habits streamlines daily routines, enhancing efficiency and productivity.
2. Personal Growth: Cultivating positive habits fosters continuous self-improvement and personal development.
3. Well-being: Breaking negative habits improves mental, emotional, and physical well-being, promoting a healthier lifestyle.
4. Goal Achievement: Habit mastery supports goal achievement by aligning daily actions with long-term aspirations and values.

By harnessing the power of habits through intentional behavior change and consistent practice, individuals can shape their lives in alignment with their goals and values. Whether forming positive habits or breaking negative ones, understanding habit dynamics and employing effective strategies empowers individuals to cultivate a fulfilling and balanced life.

Chapter 70: Understanding Relationships

Building Strong Personal Connections

Building and maintaining strong personal connections enriches life satisfaction and emotional well-being, fostering meaningful relationships.

1. Foundations of Healthy Relationships:

- Trust and Communication: Establish trust through open, honest communication and active listening.

- Respect and Empathy: Show respect for differences and cultivate empathy to understand others' perspectives.

2. Key Elements of Strong Relationships:
   - Support: Offer and receive emotional support, encouragement, and companionship during both joyful and challenging times.
   - Shared Values: Share common values, interests, and goals that strengthen the bond and foster mutual understanding.

Navigating Complex Relationships

1. Types of Relationships:
 - Family Dynamics: Navigate familial relationships with sensitivity to roles, expectations, and generational differences.
   - Friendships: Cultivate friendships based on mutual respect, shared interests, and supportive interactions.

2. Challenges in Relationships:
   - Conflict Resolution: Develop skills for resolving conflicts constructively, respecting differing viewpoints, and finding mutually agreeable solutions.
   - Boundaries: Establish and maintain healthy boundaries to protect personal well-being and promote mutual respect.

3. Building Resilient Relationships:
   - Adaptability: Embrace change and adaptability to navigate transitions and challenges within relationships.
   - Forgiveness: Practice forgiveness and acceptance to overcome conflicts and strengthen emotional bonds.

Benefits of Strong Relationships

1. Emotional Support: Receive empathy, encouragement, and understanding, which enhances emotional resilience and well-being.
2. Social Connection: Combat feelings of loneliness and isolation by fostering meaningful connections and a sense of belonging.

3. Personal Growth: Learn from diverse perspectives, experiences, and feedback within relationships, fostering continuous personal growth.

4. Health and Well-being: Improve physical health and longevity through positive social interactions and support networks.

By prioritizing communication, empathy, and mutual respect, individuals can cultivate strong, resilient relationships that enrich their lives and contribute to overall happiness and well-being. Navigating complex dynamics with understanding and adaptability fosters deeper connections and promotes harmony within personal and social spheres.

Chapter 71: The Role of Empathy

Understanding and Sharing Emotions

Empathy plays a crucial role in interpersonal relationships and emotional intelligence, facilitating understanding and connection through shared emotions.

1. Definition of Empathy:
   - Emotional Understanding: Empathy involves recognizing, understanding, and sharing the emotions and perspectives of others.
   - Compassionate Response: Responding to others' emotions with compassion, sensitivity, and support.

2. Types of Empathy:
   - Cognitive Empathy: Understanding another person's emotions intellectually by perceiving their perspective.
   - Emotional Empathy: Feeling and sharing another person's emotions as if they were your own, demonstrating emotional resonance.

Cultivating Empathy in Interactions

1. Active Listening:

- Presence: Be fully present and attentive during conversations, focusing on understanding the speaker's feelings and thoughts.
- Non-verbal Cues: Pay attention to non-verbal cues such as facial expressions, body language, and tone of voice to discern emotions.

2. Perspective-Taking:
- Putting Yourself in Their Shoes: Imagine yourself in the other person's situation to gain insight into their emotions and experiences.
- Empathic Imagination: Use creative empathy exercises to deepen understanding and foster empathy skills.

3. Validation and Support:
- Acknowledgement: Validate and acknowledge the other person's emotions and experiences without judgment.
- Offering Support: Provide emotional support and reassurance, showing empathy through actions that demonstrate care and understanding.

Benefits of Empathy

1. Enhanced Relationships: Strengthen interpersonal connections by fostering trust, mutual respect, and emotional intimacy.
2. Conflict Resolution: Facilitate constructive conflict resolution by understanding differing perspectives and finding common ground.
3. Emotional Intelligence: Develop emotional intelligence by managing and expressing emotions effectively, both personally and in relationships.
4. Community and Societal Impact: Promote compassion and cooperation within communities, contributing to a more empathetic and supportive society.

By actively cultivating empathy in interactions and relationships, individuals can foster deeper connections, emotional resilience, and personal growth. Empathy serves as a bridge that enhances understanding, compassion, and collaboration, ultimately enriching both personal and social dynamics.

The Wisdom of Discernment
Navigating Life's Good and Bad

Chapter 72: Dealing with Criticism

Receiving Constructive Feedback

Learning to receive constructive feedback positively is essential for personal and professional growth, fostering self-improvement and learning from others' perspectives.

1. Approach to Constructive Feedback:
   - Openness: Approach feedback with an open mind and willingness to learn, viewing it as an opportunity for growth.
   - Active Listening: Listen attentively to understand the feedback giver's perspective and insights.
   - Reflect and Evaluate: Take time to reflect on the feedback and evaluate its validity and potential for improvement.

2. Responding to Constructive Feedback:
   - Gratitude: Express appreciation for the feedback, acknowledging the effort taken to provide insights.
   - Action Plan: Develop an action plan to address areas for improvement identified through feedback.
   - Follow-up: Seek clarification if needed and provide updates on progress made based on the feedback received.

Responding to Negative Criticism

1. Managing Emotional Responses:
   - Stay Calm: Maintain composure and avoid reacting impulsively or defensively.
   - Pause and Reflect: Take a moment to process the criticism before responding, focusing on understanding the underlying reasons.

2. Analyzing Negative Criticism:
   - Separate Emotion from Content: Focus on the substance of the criticism rather than the tone or delivery.

The Wisdom of Discernment
Navigating Life's Good and Bad

- Seek Clarification: Ask for specific examples or details to better understand the criticism and its implications.

3. Turning Negative Criticism into Opportunities:
  - Learning Opportunity: Extract lessons or insights from the criticism to facilitate personal growth and improvement.
  - Addressing Valid Points: Acknowledge valid points raised and develop strategies to address them constructively.

4. Maintaining Perspective:
  - Consider the Source: Evaluate the credibility and intentions of the critic to contextualize the feedback appropriately.
  - Self-Reflection: Reflect on personal responses and behaviors to identify areas for adjustment or improvement.

Benefits of Effective Criticism Handling

1. Personal Growth: Foster continuous improvement and self-awareness through constructive feedback and reflection.
2. Professional Development: Enhance professional skills and performance by addressing areas for growth identified through feedback.
3. Enhanced Relationships: Strengthen interpersonal relationships by demonstrating openness to feedback and willingness to learn from others.

By developing skills to receive and respond to criticism effectively, individuals can leverage feedback as a catalyst for growth and improvement, both personally and professionally. Embracing feedback—whether constructive or negative—empowers individuals to refine their abilities, enhance relationships, and achieve their full potential.

Chapter 73: Overcoming Procrastination

Identifying Procrastination Triggers

The Wisdom of Discernment

Navigating Life's Good and Bad

Understanding the root causes of procrastination is key to overcoming this common challenge and enhancing productivity.

1. Common Procrastination Triggers:

  - Fear of Failure: Avoiding tasks due to anxiety about not meeting expectations or making mistakes.

  - Lack of Clarity: Uncertainty about where to start or how to approach a task can lead to avoidance.

  - Perfectionism: Setting excessively high standards that can result in delaying tasks until conditions feel ideal.

  - Task Aversion: Disliking or feeling overwhelmed by certain tasks, leading to avoidance behavior.

2. Self-Assessment and Awareness:

  - Reflective Practice: Take time to self-assess and identify recurring patterns or situations that trigger procrastination.

  - Mindfulness: Cultivate mindfulness to recognize when procrastination tendencies arise and their underlying causes.

Techniques to Stay Productive

1. Goal Setting and Planning:

  - SMART Goals: Define Specific, Measurable, Achievable, Relevant, and Time-bound goals to provide clarity and motivation.

  - Prioritization: Use techniques like Eisenhower Matrix to prioritize tasks based on urgency and importance.

2. Time Management Strategies:

  - Pomodoro Technique: Break tasks into intervals with short breaks to maintain focus and productivity.

  - Time Blocking: Allocate specific time slots for tasks, minimizing distractions and increasing efficiency.

The Wisdom of Discernment
Navigating Life's Good and Bad

3. Mindset and Motivation:

- Chunking: Break tasks into smaller, manageable steps to reduce overwhelm and build momentum.

- Visualization: Visualize completing tasks and the benefits of accomplishing them to enhance motivation.

4. Accountability and Support:

- Accountability Partners: Share goals and progress with a trusted friend or colleague to stay accountable.

- Support Networks: Seek encouragement and guidance from peers or mentors to stay motivated during challenging tasks.

Overcoming Procrastination for Long-term Success

1. Building Consistent Habits:

- Routine: Establish a daily or weekly routine that includes dedicated time for important tasks.

- Progress Tracking: Monitor and celebrate progress to reinforce positive behaviors and build momentum.

2. Learning and Adaptation:

- Continuous Improvement: Learn from setbacks and adjust strategies to optimize productivity over time.

- Flexibility: Embrace adaptability to handle unexpected challenges and maintain productivity.

3. Self-Care and Well-being:

- Rest and Recovery: Prioritize adequate rest and breaks to maintain energy levels and prevent burnout.

- Health and Wellness: Support productivity with healthy habits, such as exercise, nutrition, and sufficient sleep.

By implementing these strategies and cultivating self-awareness, individuals can overcome procrastination, enhance productivity, and achieve their goals with greater efficiency and satisfaction. Embracing proactive habits and maintaining a positive mindset empower individuals to navigate challenges effectively and sustain long-term success.

Chapter 74: Financial Literacy

Basics of Personal Finance

Understanding the fundamentals of personal finance is essential for making informed financial decisions and achieving long-term financial security.

1. Budgeting and Financial Planning:
  - Income and Expenses: Track income sources and expenses to create a budget that aligns with financial goals.
   - Saving and Spending: Prioritize saving by allocating funds for essentials, discretionary spending, and savings goals.
  - Emergency Fund: Establish an emergency fund to cover unexpected expenses and financial emergencies.

2. Debt Management:
  - Types of Debt: Differentiate between good debt (e.g., education loans) and bad debt (e.g., high-interest credit card debt).
   - Debt Repayment Strategies: Develop a plan to pay off debts systematically, focusing on high-interest debts first.

3. Investing Basics:
   - Types of Investments: Understand various investment options, such as stocks, bonds, mutual funds, and real estate.
  - Risk and Return: Evaluate risk tolerance and investment goals to make informed decisions about asset allocation.

Planning for Financial Future

The Wisdom of Discernment
Navigating Life's Good and Bad

1. Setting Financial Goals:
   - Short-term and Long-term Goals: Define specific financial goals, such as buying a home, saving for retirement, or funding education.
   - SMART Goals: Ensure goals are Specific, Measurable, Achievable, Relevant, and Time-bound to maintain focus and track progress.

2. Retirement Planning:
   - Retirement Accounts: Explore retirement savings options like employer-sponsored plans (e.g., 401(k)) and Individual Retirement Accounts (IRAs).
   - Investment Strategies: Develop a diversified investment portfolio tailored to retirement goals and time horizon.

3. Risk Management:
   - Insurance Coverage: Evaluate insurance needs, including health, life, disability, and property insurance, to protect against financial risks.
   - Estate Planning: Prepare for the future by creating a will, establishing powers of attorney, and outlining healthcare directives.

Financial Education and Empowerment

1. Continuous Learning:
   - Financial Literacy Resources: Access educational materials, workshops, and online resources to enhance financial knowledge and skills.
   - Professional Advice: Consult financial advisors or planners for personalized guidance on complex financial matters.

2. Behavioral Finance:
   - Understanding Financial Behavior: Recognize behavioral biases and psychological factors that influence financial decisions.
   - Behavior Modification: Implement strategies to overcome emotional biases and make rational financial choices.

3. Financial Well-being:
 - Balancing Financial and Personal Goals: Integrate financial decisions with personal values and life priorities to achieve overall well-being.
 - Long-term Financial Security: Foster financial resilience and prepare for economic fluctuations by adopting prudent financial practices.

By mastering the basics of personal finance and planning for the future, individuals can build a solid foundation for financial well-being and achieve their financial aspirations with confidence and clarity. Empowering oneself with financial literacy equips individuals to navigate economic challenges, seize opportunities, and cultivate financial independence over the long term.

Chapter 75: Personal Branding

Defining Your Personal Brand

Personal branding is about crafting a distinct identity and reputation that communicates your unique strengths, values, and goals to others.

1. Self-Reflection and Assessment:
 - Identify Your Strengths: Reflect on your skills, experiences, and passions to define what sets you apart from others.
 - Clarify Your Values: Determine your core values and beliefs that guide your decisions and actions.

2. Defining Your Unique Proposition:
 - Mission Statement: Create a concise statement that encapsulates your purpose, what you offer, and who you serve.
 - Brand Personality: Develop a persona that reflects your authentic self and resonates with your target audience.

Building and Promoting Your Brand

1. Consistent Brand Messaging:
   - Brand Voice: Establish a consistent tone and style in your communication that aligns with your brand identity.
   - Visual Identity: Design a cohesive visual identity with a logo, color palette, and typography that reflects your brand personality.

2. Online Presence and Networking:
   - Digital Footprint: Manage your online presence across social media platforms, websites, and professional networks.
   - Content Creation: Share valuable insights, expertise, and experiences through blogs, articles, videos, and podcasts to establish thought leadership.

3. Networking and Relationship Building:
   - Professional Relationships: Build meaningful connections with peers, mentors, industry leaders, and potential collaborators.
   - Networking Events: Attend industry conferences, seminars, and networking events to expand your professional circle and visibility.

Leveraging Your Personal Brand

1. Differentiation and Value Proposition:
   - Unique Selling Proposition (USP): Highlight what makes you unique and valuable to employers, clients, or collaborators.
   - Competitive Advantage: Position yourself as an expert in your field by showcasing your knowledge, skills, and achievements.

2. Continuous Growth and Adaptation:
   - Professional Development: Invest in ongoing learning and skill development to stay relevant and competitive in your industry.
   - Feedback and Iteration: Seek feedback from peers and mentors to refine and enhance your personal brand over time.

3. Impact and Influence:

The Wisdom of Discernment
Navigating Life's Good and Bad

- Thought Leadership: Share insights and perspectives that contribute to industry conversations and demonstrate your expertise.
- Community Engagement: Engage with your audience and community through meaningful interactions and contributions.

Personal Branding for Career Success

Personal branding empowers individuals to shape their professional identity, enhance visibility, and build credibility in their chosen field. By defining and promoting a compelling personal brand, individuals can attract opportunities, establish a strong professional reputation, and achieve long-term career success with authenticity and purpose.

Chapter 76: Ethics and Integrity

Living According to Ethical Principles

Ethics and integrity form the foundation of personal and professional conduct, guiding individuals to make principled decisions and uphold moral standards.

1. Understanding Ethical Principles:
   - Ethical Frameworks: Explore different ethical theories (e.g., deontology, consequentialism) to understand moral reasoning.
   - Core Values: Identify personal and professional values that serve as ethical guidelines in decision-making.

2. Practicing Ethical Behavior:
   - Ethical Decision-Making: Apply ethical principles to evaluate the consequences and implications of actions.
   - Accountability: Take responsibility for your decisions and actions, considering their impact on stakeholders and society.

Building a Reputation of Integrity

Integrity is the consistency between one's actions, values, and principles, essential for establishing trust and credibility in personal and professional relationships.

1. Demonstrating Integrity:
  - Honesty and Transparency: Communicate openly and truthfully, maintaining integrity in all interactions and transactions.
  - Reliability: Fulfill commitments and obligations consistently, demonstrating dependability and trustworthiness.

2. Ethical Leadership:
  - Leading by Example: Role model ethical behavior and values to inspire trust and respect among peers and subordinates.
  - Ethical Decision-Making: Encourage ethical decision-making processes within organizations and teams.

Upholding Ethical Standards

1. Ethics in Professional Settings:
  - Corporate Ethics: Adhere to organizational codes of conduct and industry regulations to promote ethical practices.
  - Conflict Resolution: Resolve ethical dilemmas through dialogue, negotiation, and mediation, prioritizing fairness and justice.

2. Personal and Professional Alignment:
  - Ethical Self-awareness: Continuously reflect on personal ethics and values to ensure alignment with professional responsibilities.
  - Continuous Learning: Stay informed about ethical issues and evolving standards in your field to adapt and uphold integrity.

Impact of Ethics and Integrity

1. Trust and Credibility:

- Building Trust: Foster trust-based relationships with stakeholders, clients, and colleagues through consistent ethical behavior.

 - Enhancing Reputation: Cultivate a reputation for integrity that enhances career opportunities and organizational success.

2. Long-term Success and Sustainability:
 - Sustainable Practices: Integrate ethical considerations into decision-making processes to promote long-term success and sustainability.
 - Social Responsibility: Contribute positively to society by prioritizing ethical conduct and responsible citizenship.

By embracing ethics and integrity as guiding principles in personal and professional life, individuals can foster a culture of trust, respect, and accountability. Upholding ethical standards not only strengthens relationships and enhances reputation but also contributes to a more ethical and sustainable society.

Chapter 77: The Role of Technology

Leveraging Technology for Good

Technology plays a transformative role in modern society, enabling innovation, connectivity, and efficiency when used responsibly and ethically.

1. Advantages of Technology:
 - Innovation: Explore how technology drives innovation across industries, from healthcare to education and beyond.
 - Connectivity: Enhance global connectivity through digital platforms, facilitating communication and collaboration.

2. Applications of Technology for Good:
 - Social Impact: Harness technology to address societal challenges such as healthcare access, education disparities, and environmental sustainability.

The Wisdom of Discernment

Navigating Life's Good and Bad

- Empowerment: Empower individuals and communities through access to information, resources, and opportunities.

Managing Technology Overuse

While technology offers numerous benefits, it's essential to maintain a balanced approach and mitigate potential drawbacks associated with overuse and dependency.

1. Awareness and Mindful Consumption:
- Digital Well-being: Practice mindful use of technology to maintain mental and emotional well-being, setting boundaries for screen time and digital interactions.
- Tech Addiction: Recognize signs of technology addiction and implement strategies for moderation and healthy usage habits.

2. Promoting Digital Citizenship:
- Ethical Use: Educate individuals on responsible digital citizenship, emphasizing respect, privacy, and cybersecurity best practices.
- Critical Thinking: Develop critical thinking skills to evaluate information sources and navigate digital content responsibly.

Ethical Considerations in Technology

1. Data Privacy and Security:
- Protecting Personal Information: Safeguard data privacy and security through encryption, secure networks, and compliance with regulations (e.g., GDPR, CCPA).
- Transparency: Advocate for transparency in data collection, usage, and consent processes to build trust with users.

2. Environmental Impact:
- Sustainability: Address the environmental impact of technology by promoting energy-efficient practices, recycling electronic waste, and supporting green initiatives.
- Carbon Footprint: Measure and reduce the carbon footprint of digital technologies through sustainable design and operational practices.

Future Trends and Innovations

1. Emerging Technologies:
   - Artificial Intelligence: Explore the potential of AI in enhancing decision-making, automation, and personalized experiences while addressing ethical concerns.
   - Blockchain: Investigate applications of blockchain technology in enhancing transparency, security, and efficiency across various sectors.

2. Human-Centered Design:
   - User Experience: Prioritize user-centric design principles to create intuitive and inclusive digital experiences that prioritize accessibility and usability.
   - Tech for All: Bridge the digital divide by promoting equal access to technology and digital literacy skills, ensuring inclusivity and equity.

Conclusion

Technology offers unprecedented opportunities for innovation, connectivity, and positive societal impact when approached with responsibility, ethics, and foresight. By leveraging technology for good while managing potential risks and challenges, individuals and organizations can contribute to a sustainable digital future that benefits all.

Chapter 78: Building a Support Network

Identifying Key Supporters

Building a robust support network is crucial for personal and professional growth, providing encouragement, guidance, and resources along the journey.

1. Identifying Key Supporters:
   - Personal Mentors: Identify mentors who offer wisdom, advice, and perspective based on their experiences and expertise.

- Friends and Family: Recognize the importance of emotional support and encouragement from loved ones who understand your aspirations.

2. Professional Networks:

- Colleagues and Peers: Cultivate relationships with colleagues and peers within your industry or field who can provide insights, collaboration opportunities, and professional advice.

- Industry Leaders: Connect with influential figures and thought leaders who can offer mentorship and open doors to new opportunities.

Strengthening Your Support System

A strong support system enhances resilience, provides constructive feedback, and fosters a sense of belonging and community.

1. Mutual Support and Reciprocity:

- Give and Receive: Build relationships based on mutual respect and reciprocity, offering support and assistance to others within your network.

- Community Engagement: Participate actively in professional associations, community groups, or online forums to expand your support network.

2. Effective Communication and Trust:

- Open Communication: Foster trust and transparency by communicating openly and honestly with your supporters about your goals, challenges, and achievements.

- Conflict Resolution: Address conflicts or misunderstandings promptly and respectfully to maintain healthy relationships within your network.

Nurturing Supportive Relationships

1. Continuous Learning and Growth:

- Feedback and Reflection: Seek feedback from your supporters to gain valuable insights and perspectives for personal and professional development.

The Wisdom of Discernment

Navigating Life's Good and Bad

- Learning Opportunities: Embrace opportunities for skill development, networking events, and workshops recommended by your support network.

2. Emotional and Practical Support:
   - Emotional Resilience: Lean on your support system during challenging times, drawing strength from their encouragement and belief in your capabilities.
   - Practical Assistance: Tap into your network for practical assistance, such as job referrals, introductions to potential collaborators, or advice on career transitions.

Impact of a Supportive Network

1. Career Advancement:
   - Professional Growth: Access career opportunities, mentorship, and industry insights that accelerate your career progression.
   - Job Satisfaction: Enhance job satisfaction by cultivating a supportive work environment and collaborative partnerships.

2. Personal Well-being:
   - Mental Health: Promote mental well-being through meaningful connections and shared experiences that reduce stress and foster a sense of belonging.
   - Work-Life Balance: Achieve balance by leveraging your support network for guidance on prioritizing personal and professional commitments effectively.

Conclusion

Building and nurturing a support network is essential for navigating life's challenges, achieving goals, and maintaining overall well-being. By cultivating genuine connections, offering support to others, and embracing opportunities for growth and collaboration, individuals can create a resilient and fulfilling support system that empowers them to thrive personally and professionally.

Chapter 79: The Importance of Play

Incorporating Play into Adult Life

Play is not just for children; it's a vital component of adult life that promotes creativity, relaxation, and overall well-being.

1. Rediscovering Playfulness:
   - Mindset Shift: Embrace a playful mindset by engaging in activities that bring joy, laughter, and spontaneity into your daily routine.
   - Exploration: Try new hobbies, games, or recreational activities to rediscover the sense of curiosity and adventure associated with play.

2. Balancing Responsibilities and Leisure:
   - Time Management: Allocate time for play amidst work and responsibilities to recharge and rejuvenate your mind and body.
   - Stress Relief: Use play as a stress-relief strategy to unwind, reduce tension, and enhance mental clarity.

Benefits of Playfulness

1. Enhanced Creativity and Innovation:
   - Creative Exploration: Foster creativity through playful experimentation and exploration of ideas, leading to innovative solutions and perspectives.
   - Problem-Solving Skills: Develop adaptive problem-solving skills by approaching challenges with a playful and flexible mindset.

2. Improved Mental and Emotional Health:
   - Stress Reduction: Lower stress levels and promote relaxation through enjoyable activities that stimulate positive emotions and laughter.
   - Mood Elevation: Boost mood and emotional resilience by engaging in playful interactions and experiences that foster connection and social bonding.

Play as a Social and Cultural Phenomenon

The Wisdom of Discernment
Navigating Life's Good and Bad

1. Social Connection and Communication:

   - Building Relationships: Strengthen social bonds and foster meaningful connections through shared play experiences and collaborative activities.

   - Team Building: Enhance teamwork and communication skills by participating in playful group activities that encourage cooperation and camaraderie.

2. Cultural and Historical Significance:

   - Cultural Traditions: Explore the role of play in cultural traditions, rituals, and celebrations that promote community cohesion and identity.

   - Historical Perspectives: Examine the evolution of play throughout history and its influence on art, literature, and societal norms.

Promoting Playfulness in Everyday Life

1. Self-Expression and Authenticity:

   - Personal Development: Express your authentic self and personality through playful expressions of creativity, humor, and imagination.

   - Self-Care: Prioritize self-care by integrating playful activities that nurture your inner child and promote holistic well-being.

2. Continued Learning and Growth:

   - Lifelong Learning: Cultivate a lifelong love for learning and discovery through playful exploration of interests, hobbies, and intellectual pursuits.

   - Adaptability: Enhance adaptability and resilience by embracing uncertainty and change with a playful and adaptive mindset.

Conclusion

Incorporating play into adult life is essential for promoting creativity, reducing stress, fostering social connections, and enhancing overall quality of life. By embracing a playful attitude and integrating enjoyable activities into daily routines, individuals can cultivate a balanced and fulfilling lifestyle that nurtures mental, emotional, and social well-being.

The Wisdom of Discernment
Navigating Life's Good and Bad

Chapter 80: Conflict Management

Resolving Disagreements Effectively

Conflict is a natural part of human interaction, and effective conflict management skills are essential for maintaining positive relationships and fostering constructive outcomes.

1. Understanding Conflict:
  - Nature of Conflict: Recognize that conflict arises from differences in perspectives, values, and goals among individuals or groups.
  - Types of Conflict: Identify different types of conflict, such as interpersonal conflicts, organizational conflicts, and cultural conflicts.

2. Effective Conflict Resolution Strategies:
  - Communication: Foster open and honest communication to clarify misunderstandings, express concerns, and listen actively to different viewpoints.
  - Collaboration: Encourage collaborative problem-solving approaches that prioritize mutual understanding and finding win-win solutions.

Maintaining Harmony

1. Promoting Positive Communication:
  - Respectful Dialogue: Maintain respect and civility during discussions, focusing on issues rather than personal attacks.
  - Active Listening: Practice active listening techniques to demonstrate empathy and understanding of others' perspectives.

2. Conflict Resolution Processes:
  - Negotiation: Use negotiation techniques to find compromises and agreements that satisfy the needs and interests of all parties involved.
  - Mediation: Utilize mediation by a neutral third party to facilitate constructive dialogue and resolution in more complex conflicts.

Building Resilient Relationships

1. Conflict Prevention and Management:
 - Early Intervention: Address conflicts early on to prevent escalation and minimize negative impacts on relationships and productivity.
  - Conflict Resolution Skills: Equip individuals and teams with conflict resolution skills through training and development programs.

2. Cultural Sensitivity and Diversity:
 - Cultural Competence: Respect cultural differences and diversity in perspectives when managing conflicts across multicultural and global contexts.
 - Inclusive Practices: Foster inclusive practices that promote equity and fairness in conflict resolution processes.

Impact of Effective Conflict Management

1. Enhanced Collaboration and Productivity:
  - Team Dynamics: Improve team cohesion and collaboration by resolving conflicts constructively and leveraging diverse strengths and perspectives.
 - Workplace Culture: Cultivate a positive workplace culture where open communication and mutual respect contribute to organizational success.

2. Personal Growth and Development:
 - Conflict Resolution Skills: Develop personal resilience and emotional intelligence through learning and practicing effective conflict resolution strategies.
  - Leadership Effectiveness: Enhance leadership effectiveness by demonstrating competence in managing conflicts and promoting a culture of accountability and trust.

Conclusion

Effective conflict management is crucial for promoting harmonious relationships, fostering collaboration, and achieving positive outcomes in personal and professional settings. By embracing proactive communication, respectful dialogue, and collaborative problem-solving approaches, individuals and organizations can navigate conflicts constructively and cultivate environments where mutual respect and understanding prevail.

Chapter 81: Cultivating Creativity

Unlocking Creative Potential

Creativity is a valuable skill that can be nurtured and developed through deliberate practice and a conducive environment.

1. Understanding Creativity:
    - Definition: Define creativity as the ability to generate novel ideas, solutions, or expressions that are original and valuable.
    - Importance: Recognize the significance of creativity in problem-solving, innovation, and personal fulfillment.

2. Factors Influencing Creativity:
    - Mindset: Adopt a growth mindset that embraces challenges, persistence, and learning from failures as essential components of the creative process.
    - Environment: Create an environment that stimulates creativity, such as spaces that inspire, freedom to experiment, and exposure to diverse perspectives and stimuli.

Nurturing Creativity in Daily Life

1. Creative Practices and Habits:
    - Brainstorming: Engage in brainstorming sessions to generate multiple ideas without judgment or self-censorship.
    - Mind Mapping: Use mind mapping techniques to visualize connections and associations between ideas, fostering creativity and innovation.

2. Creative Exercises and Activities:
    - Divergent Thinking: Practice divergent thinking exercises to explore multiple possibilities and unconventional solutions to problems.

- Creative Challenges: Set creative challenges or prompts to spark creativity and encourage experimentation with different approaches and techniques.

Integrating Creativity into Work and Personal Projects

1. Creativity in Problem-Solving:
   - Creative Problem-Solving: Apply creative problem-solving techniques, such as lateral thinking and reframing, to overcome challenges and find innovative solutions.
   - Design Thinking: Utilize design thinking methodologies to empathize with users, define problems, ideate solutions, prototype ideas, and iterate based on feedback.

2. Expressive and Artistic Outlets:
   - Artistic Expression: Explore artistic outlets, such as painting, writing, music, or theater, to channel emotions, express ideas, and stimulate creative thinking.
   - Creative Writing: Engage in creative writing exercises, storytelling, or journaling to enhance narrative skills and develop a unique voice.

Cultivating a Creative Mindset

1. Continuous Learning and Inspiration:
   - Curiosity: Cultivate curiosity and a thirst for knowledge by exploring new interests, reading diverse literature, and engaging with different cultures and perspectives.
   - Inspiration Sources: Seek inspiration from nature, art, literature, music, and everyday experiences that provoke thought and ignite creative ideas.

2. Collaboration and Feedback:
   - Collaborative Creativity: Collaborate with others to exchange ideas, receive feedback, and co-create innovative solutions that leverage diverse expertise and perspectives.
   - Constructive Feedback: Embrace constructive feedback to refine and improve creative work, fostering growth and development in creative endeavors.

Conclusion

The Wisdom of Discernment
Navigating Life's Good and Bad

Cultivating creativity involves unlocking your creative potential through mindset shifts, nurturing creative habits, and integrating creative practices into your daily life. By fostering an environment that encourages experimentation, embraces diversity of thought, and values the creative process, individuals can harness their creativity to generate novel ideas, solve complex problems, and enrich both personal and professional endeavors.

Chapter 82: Travel and Exploration

Benefits of Exploring New Places

Traveling and exploring new places offer numerous benefits that enrich personal growth, broaden perspectives, and foster cultural understanding.

1. Cultural Immersion and Diversity:
   - Experiencing New Cultures: Immerse yourself in different cultures, traditions, and lifestyles to gain insights into global diversity and interconnectedness.
   - Cultural Exchange: Engage with locals, participate in cultural activities, and sample local cuisine to deepen your understanding and appreciation of diverse customs and perspectives.

2. Personal Growth and Development:
   - Self-Discovery: Embark on journeys of self-discovery and personal reflection as you navigate unfamiliar environments and encounter new challenges.
   - Adaptability: Cultivate adaptability and resilience by navigating language barriers, logistical challenges, and cultural norms in diverse settings.

Planning Meaningful Travel Experiences

1. Setting Intentions and Goals:
   - Purposeful Travel: Define your travel goals and intentions, whether it's to explore historical sites, pursue outdoor adventures, or engage in volunteerism and cultural exchange.
   - Bucket List: Create a bucket list of destinations and experiences that align with your interests, values, and aspirations for meaningful travel.

2. Practical Considerations and Preparation:

- Research and Preparation: Conduct thorough research on destinations, including safety considerations, visa requirements, local customs, and sustainable travel practices.

- Itinerary Planning: Develop a flexible itinerary that balances structured activities with opportunities for spontaneity and serendipitous discoveries.

Embracing Exploration as a Lifestyle

1. Mindful Travel and Sustainability:

- Responsible Tourism: Practice responsible tourism by minimizing environmental impact, supporting local economies, and respecting cultural heritage and natural resources.

- Sustainable Practices: Reduce carbon footprint through eco-friendly transportation, accommodations, and consumption choices during travel.

2. Learning and Cultural Exchange:

- Educational Opportunities: Expand your knowledge and global perspective through educational tours, museum visits, guided excursions, and interactions with local experts.

- Language Skills: Enhance language skills by immersing yourself in local dialects, phrases, and conversational exchanges with native speakers.

Enriching Experiences and Memories

1. Social Connections and Networking:

- Building Relationships: Foster meaningful connections with fellow travelers, locals, and hosts to exchange stories, share experiences, and forge lifelong friendships.

- Community Engagement: Participate in community-based initiatives, volunteer programs, or cultural exchanges that contribute positively to local communities and promote social responsibility.

2. Reflection and Integration:

- Reflective Practices: Journaling, photography, and storytelling to capture memories, insights, and lessons learned from travel experiences.

The Wisdom of Discernment
Navigating Life's Good and Bad

- Integration: Apply newfound perspectives, skills, and cultural knowledge gained from travel to enrich personal and professional endeavors upon returning home.

Conclusion

Travel and exploration offer transformative opportunities for cultural immersion, personal growth, and global citizenship. By planning meaningful travel experiences, embracing diverse cultures, and practicing responsible tourism, individuals can cultivate empathy, resilience, and a deeper appreciation for the interconnectedness of our world. Travel not only broadens horizons but also inspires lifelong learning, fosters cross-cultural understanding, and creates enduring memories that enrich the fabric of our lives.

Chapter 83: Finding Your Passion

Discovering What Drives You

Finding your passion involves identifying activities, interests, and pursuits that ignite your enthusiasm, align with your values, and bring a sense of purpose and fulfillment to your life.

1. Self-Exploration and Reflection:
   - Identifying Interests: Reflect on activities and experiences that evoke joy, curiosity, and a sense of flow, indicating potential areas of passion.
   - Core Values: Align your passions with your core values and beliefs to ensure they resonate authentically with who you are and what you stand for.

2. Exploring Different Paths:
   - Experimentation: Try new hobbies, explore diverse fields of study, and engage in experiential learning to discover new passions and interests.
   - Career Exploration: Assess how your passions can translate into meaningful careers or entrepreneurial ventures that align with your professional goals and aspirations.

Pursuing Passion Projects

The Wisdom of Discernment
Navigating Life's Good and Bad

1. Setting Goals and Intentions:

- Goal Clarity: Define clear goals and objectives for your passion projects, whether it's mastering a skill, launching a creative endeavor, or making a positive impact in your community.

- Action Planning: Develop actionable steps and timelines to progress towards your goals, breaking down larger projects into manageable tasks.

2. Overcoming Challenges and Obstacles:

- Resilience: Cultivate resilience and perseverance to navigate setbacks, challenges, and self-doubt that may arise during the pursuit of your passion.

- Learning from Failure: Embrace failure as a natural part of growth and use setbacks as opportunities for learning, adaptation, and improvement.

Integrating Passion into Daily Life

1. Work-Life Integration:

- Balance: Strive for balance by integrating your passions into your daily routines, work commitments, and personal life to maintain well-being and fulfillment.

- Time Management: Prioritize time for passion projects, leveraging productivity techniques and effective time management strategies to maximize creative output.

2. Sharing and Collaboration:

- Community Engagement: Engage with like-minded individuals, join communities, or collaborate with peers who share your passions to exchange ideas, gain support, and foster mutual inspiration.

- Mentorship: Seek mentorship from experienced individuals in your field of interest to gain insights, guidance, and encouragement in pursuing your passion projects.

Sustaining Motivation and Growth

1. Continuous Learning and Development:

- Skill Enhancement: Commit to ongoing learning, skill development, and mastery in your chosen passion areas to deepen expertise and stay motivated.

The Wisdom of Discernment
Navigating Life's Good and Bad

- Personal Growth: Embrace personal growth opportunities through reflection, feedback, and self-improvement to evolve as both a passionate individual and a lifelong learner.

2. Celebrating Achievements and Milestones:
   - Recognition: Celebrate milestones, achievements, and successes along your passion journey to reinforce motivation, boost morale, and inspire further creativity.
   - Gratitude: Practice gratitude for the opportunity to pursue your passions, acknowledging the support of others and the fulfillment derived from living a purpose-driven life.

Conclusion

Finding your passion involves a journey of self-discovery, exploration, and commitment to pursuing activities that bring joy, meaning, and fulfillment to your life. By aligning your passions with your values, setting clear goals, overcoming challenges, and integrating passion into your daily routines, you can cultivate a life enriched with purpose, creativity, and personal growth. Embrace the process of discovering what drives you, nurturing your passions, and contributing your unique talents and energies to make a positive impact on yourself and the world around you.

Chapter 84: Public Speaking

Overcoming Fear of Speaking

Public speaking is a valuable skill that can be developed through practice, preparation, and mindset shifts to overcome fear and anxiety associated with speaking in front of an audience.

1. Understanding Fear of Public Speaking:
   - Identifying Anxiety Triggers: Recognize common triggers such as fear of judgment, performance anxiety, or lack of confidence in public speaking abilities.
   - Mindset Shifts: Adopt a growth mindset by reframing fear as excitement and viewing public speaking as an opportunity for personal and professional growth.

2. Techniques for Managing Anxiety:

- Breathing Exercises: Practice deep breathing techniques to calm nerves and reduce physical symptoms of anxiety before and during public speaking engagements.

- Visualization: Use visualization techniques to mentally rehearse successful speaking scenarios, visualize a supportive audience, and envision positive outcomes.

Mastering Public Speaking Skills

1. Effective Preparation and Practice:
 - Research and Content Development: Conduct thorough research on your topic, organize key points logically, and develop engaging content that resonates with your audience.
 - Rehearsal: Rehearse your speech or presentation multiple times to refine delivery, timing, and emphasis on key messages while familiarizing yourself with the flow of your presentation.

2. Engaging Your Audience:
 - Opening Impact: Start with a compelling opening, such as a story, question, or surprising fact, to capture audience attention and establish rapport.
 - Body Language: Use confident body language, including eye contact, gestures, and posture, to convey authority, establish credibility, and maintain audience engagement.

Building Confidence and Presence

1. Confidence Building Strategies:
 - Positive Self-Talk: Replace negative thoughts with affirmations and positive self-talk to boost confidence and reinforce belief in your ability to deliver a successful presentation.
 - Gradual Exposure: Gradually expose yourself to speaking opportunities, starting with smaller groups or supportive environments, to build confidence over time.

2. Handling Q&A Sessions and Feedback:
 - Anticipate Questions: Prepare for potential questions and objections from the audience, demonstrating knowledge, clarity, and responsiveness in your responses.
 - Feedback: Seek constructive feedback from peers, mentors, or audience members to identify areas for improvement and refine your public speaking skills.

Advanced Techniques and Continuous Improvement

1. Advanced Speaking Techniques:
  - Storytelling: Incorporate storytelling techniques to convey information, evoke emotions, and make your message memorable and relatable to your audience.
  - Humor and Authenticity: Use humor, personal anecdotes, and authenticity to connect with your audience on a deeper level and enhance engagement.

2. Professional Development and Growth:
  - Professional Speaking Opportunities: Seek opportunities to speak at conferences, workshops, or community events to gain experience, expand your network, and elevate your reputation as a skilled public speaker.
  - Continual Learning: Commit to ongoing learning, attend public speaking workshops, read books on communication and presentation skills, and learn from experienced speakers to refine and enhance your speaking abilities.

Conclusion

Mastering public speaking requires overcoming fear, mastering essential skills, building confidence, and continuously refining your techniques through practice and professional development. By embracing opportunities to speak publicly, preparing effectively, engaging your audience, and seeking feedback, you can enhance your ability to communicate persuasively, influence others positively, and deliver impactful presentations that leave a lasting impression. Embrace the journey of becoming a confident and proficient public speaker, leveraging your voice to inspire, inform, and connect with audiences effectively.

Chapter 85: The Importance of Sleep

Understanding Sleep Health

Sleep is a fundamental biological need that plays a crucial role in physical health, mental well-being, cognitive function, and overall quality of life.

The Wisdom of Discernment
Navigating Life's Good and Bad

1. The Science of Sleep:
 - Sleep Cycles: Explore the stages of sleep, including REM (Rapid Eye Movement) and non-REM sleep, and their importance in restorative functions, memory consolidation, and emotional regulation.
 - Biological Rhythms: Understand circadian rhythms and the body's natural sleep-wake cycle, influenced by factors such as light exposure, hormones, and internal body clock.

2. Impact of Sleep on Health:
 - Physical Health: Highlight the role of sleep in immune function, cardiovascular health, metabolism, and disease prevention, emphasizing its contribution to overall physical well-being.
 - Mental Health: Discuss the link between sleep and mental health, including its role in mood regulation, stress management, and resilience against mental health disorders.

Developing Healthy Sleep Habits

1. Creating a Sleep-Conducive Environment:
 - Optimal Sleep Environment: Design a bedroom environment that promotes relaxation and sleep, including considerations for noise levels, temperature, and comfort.
 - Sleep Hygiene Practices: Establish bedtime routines, such as dimming lights, avoiding screens before bed, and engaging in calming activities like reading or meditation, to signal to your body that it's time to sleep.

2. Establishing Consistent Sleep Patterns:
 - Routine and Consistency: Maintain regular sleep-wake schedules, even on weekends, to synchronize circadian rhythms and improve sleep quality over time.
 - Napping Guidelines: Discuss the benefits of strategic napping while emphasizing the importance of keeping naps short and avoiding late-day naps that may disrupt nighttime sleep.

Strategies for Better Sleep Quality

1. Mind-Body Techniques:

  - Relaxation Techniques: Practice relaxation exercises, such as deep breathing, progressive muscle relaxation, or guided imagery, to reduce stress levels and prepare the mind and body for sleep.

  - Cognitive Behavioral Therapy for Insomnia (CBT-I): Explore evidence-based strategies to address underlying sleep disorders, manage sleep-related anxiety, and promote healthier sleep patterns.

2. Nutrition and Lifestyle Factors:

  - Sleep-Supportive Diet: Discuss the impact of diet on sleep quality, emphasizing the role of balanced nutrition, hydration, and mindful eating habits in promoting restful sleep.

  - Physical Activity: Highlight the benefits of regular exercise in improving sleep quality and overall well-being, while cautioning against vigorous exercise close to bedtime.

Benefits of Adequate Sleep

1. Cognitive Function and Productivity:

  - Memory and Learning: Examine how adequate sleep enhances cognitive functions such as memory consolidation, problem-solving abilities, and learning retention.

  - Daytime Alertness: Emphasize the importance of feeling refreshed and alert during waking hours, which supports productivity, concentration, and decision-making skills.

2. Emotional Resilience and Well-being:

  - Emotional Regulation: Discuss the link between sleep and emotional resilience, including its role in managing stress, regulating emotions, and promoting positive mood states.

  - Quality of Life: Highlight how sufficient, restorative sleep contributes to overall quality of life, satisfaction with daily activities, and long-term psychological well-being.

Conclusion

Understanding the importance of sleep and developing healthy sleep habits are essential for optimizing physical health, mental well-being, and overall quality of life. By prioritizing sleep hygiene practices, creating a sleep-conducive environment, and adopting strategies to enhance sleep quality, individuals can improve their sleep patterns, reap the benefits of restorative sleep, and achieve a balanced and fulfilling lifestyle. Embrace the science of sleep, prioritize your sleep health, and empower yourself to enjoy the profound benefits of a good night's rest for optimal health and well-being.

Chapter 86: Volunteerism and Giving Back

Benefits of Volunteering

Volunteerism is a powerful way to contribute to your community, make a positive impact, and experience personal growth and fulfillment through altruistic actions.

1. Personal Development and Well-being:
  - Sense of Purpose: Explore how volunteering provides a sense of purpose and fulfillment by contributing to causes that align with your values and interests.
  - Personal Growth: Discuss opportunities for personal growth, including skill development, increased self-confidence, and expanding social networks through meaningful interactions with others.

2. Health and Happiness:
  - Mental Health Benefits: Highlight the positive impact of volunteering on mental health, such as reducing stress, combating feelings of loneliness, and fostering a sense of belonging and community.
  - Physical Health: Discuss potential physical health benefits, including increased physical activity levels, improved cardiovascular health, and enhanced overall well-being.

Finding Opportunities to Give Back

1. Identifying Causes and Organizations:
  - Passion Alignment: Encourage individuals to identify causes and issues they are passionate about, whether it's environmental conservation, education, healthcare, or social justice.

The Wisdom of Discernment
Navigating Life's Good and Bad

- Research and Networking: Provide strategies for researching local nonprofits, community organizations, and volunteer opportunities through online platforms, community centers, or referrals from friends and colleagues.

2. Types of Volunteer Opportunities:

  - Direct Service: Discuss opportunities for hands-on volunteering, such as mentoring youth, serving meals at homeless shelters, or participating in community clean-up initiatives.

  - Indirect Service: Explore ways to contribute behind the scenes, such as fundraising, event planning, administrative support, or digital advocacy for nonprofit causes.

Making an Impact

1. Building Meaningful Relationships:

  - Community Engagement: Highlight the importance of building meaningful connections with fellow volunteers, beneficiaries, and community members, fostering a sense of camaraderie and shared purpose.

  - Networking and Collaboration: Discuss how volunteering can lead to professional networking opportunities, career advancement, and collaborative partnerships within the nonprofit sector.

2. Sustainability and Long-term Engagement:

  - Commitment and Consistency: Emphasize the value of sustained volunteer engagement over time, establishing reliable support for organizations and causes facing ongoing challenges.

  - Impact Assessment: Encourage reflection on personal contributions, recognizing the collective impact of volunteer efforts on individuals, communities, and society at large.

Overcoming Barriers to Volunteering

1. Time Management and Flexibility:

  - Balancing Commitments: Provide tips for integrating volunteerism into busy schedules, emphasizing flexible opportunities and remote volunteering options that accommodate diverse lifestyles.

- Skills-Based Volunteering: Promote the concept of skills-based volunteering, where individuals contribute specialized skills, expertise, or professional knowledge to support nonprofit missions effectively.

2. Inspiring Others to Volunteer:
- Advocacy and Awareness: Discuss the role of volunteer advocates in raising awareness about social issues, inspiring others to get involved, and amplifying the impact of collective efforts.
- Storytelling and Impact Sharing: Share inspiring stories of volunteerism, highlighting personal experiences, transformative moments, and the ripple effects of giving back on individuals and communities.

Conclusion

Volunteerism and giving back offer transformative opportunities to make a meaningful difference in the world while fostering personal growth, strengthening communities, and promoting social change. By embracing volunteerism, individuals can discover their passions, build valuable skills, forge connections with others, and contribute to creating a more compassionate and inclusive society. Explore the rewards of volunteering, find opportunities that resonate with your interests and values, and embark on a journey of positive impact and fulfillment through altruistic actions and community service.

Chapter 87: Leadership Development

Developing Leadership Skills

Leadership development is a continuous journey of acquiring and honing essential skills and qualities to effectively guide and inspire others towards shared goals and aspirations.

1. Core Leadership Competencies:
- Communication: Emphasize the importance of clear and effective communication in conveying vision, goals, and expectations to team members and stakeholders.

- Decision-Making: Discuss strategies for making informed and timely decisions, considering multiple perspectives, data-driven insights, and long-term implications.

2. Emotional Intelligence and Empathy:

- Self-Awareness: Encourage leaders to cultivate self-awareness, understanding their strengths, weaknesses, and emotional triggers to enhance interpersonal relationships and decision-making.

- Empathy: Highlight the role of empathy in fostering trust, understanding others' perspectives, and creating a supportive and inclusive work environment.

Leading with Compassion and Integrity

1. Ethical Leadership:

- Integrity: Define integrity as the foundation of ethical leadership, emphasizing honesty, transparency, and consistency in actions and decision-making.

- Accountability: Discuss the importance of holding oneself and others accountable for commitments, responsibilities, and ethical standards.

2. Compassionate Leadership:

- Empowerment and Support: Explore how compassionate leaders empower team members, provide mentorship, and create opportunities for growth and development.

- Resilience and Adaptability: Discuss resilience as a key trait of compassionate leaders, navigating challenges with empathy, flexibility, and a solutions-oriented mindset.

Strategies for Leadership Development

1. Continuous Learning and Growth:

- Professional Development: Encourage leaders to pursue ongoing learning opportunities, such as workshops, courses, and mentoring relationships, to expand their knowledge and leadership capabilities.

- Feedback and Reflection: Promote a culture of feedback and self-reflection, soliciting input from peers, mentors, and team members to identify strengths, areas for improvement, and growth opportunities.

The Wisdom of Discernment
Navigating Life's Good and Bad

2. Building High-Performing Teams:

- Team Collaboration: Discuss strategies for fostering collaboration, building cohesive teams, and leveraging diverse talents and perspectives to achieve collective goals.

- Conflict Resolution: Provide techniques for addressing conflicts constructively, promoting open communication, and fostering resolutions that strengthen team dynamics and productivity.

Leading Through Challenges and Change

1. Change Management:

- Adaptation and Innovation: Explore how effective leaders navigate change, inspire innovation, and guide teams through transitions with resilience, agility, and a focus on long-term goals.

- Communication Strategies: Highlight the role of transparent and empathetic communication in managing change, addressing concerns, and maintaining team morale and engagement.

2. Strategic Vision and Goal Alignment:

- Visionary Leadership: Encourage leaders to articulate a compelling vision, aligning team efforts with organizational goals, and inspiring commitment to a shared mission.

- Goal Setting and Execution: Discuss best practices for setting SMART (Specific, Measurable, Achievable, Relevant, Time-bound) goals, monitoring progress, and celebrating milestones to sustain motivation and momentum.

Conclusion

Leadership development is a transformative journey that requires dedication, self-awareness, and a commitment to continuous improvement. By developing essential leadership skills, leading with compassion and integrity, and embracing lifelong learning, leaders can inspire trust, drive innovation, and empower others to achieve collective success. Embrace the responsibilities and opportunities of leadership, foster a culture of collaboration and accountability, and lead with purpose and empathy to create positive impact and lasting change in your organization and beyond.

Chapter 88: Effective Problem-Solving

Strategies for Solving Problems

Effective problem-solving involves a systematic approach to identifying, analyzing, and resolving challenges or obstacles encountered in various aspects of life and work.

1. Define the Problem:
   - Clarity and Understanding: Emphasize the importance of clearly defining the problem statement, identifying underlying causes, and distinguishing between symptoms and root causes.
   - Problem Framing: Discuss techniques for framing problems in a way that facilitates exploration of potential solutions and considers diverse perspectives.

2. Gather Information and Analyze Data:
   - Research and Data Collection: Encourage systematic gathering of relevant information, data, and insights to understand the scope and impact of the problem.
   - Root Cause Analysis: Introduce methods such as Fishbone diagrams (Ishikawa), 5 Whys, or Pareto Analysis to identify root causes and prioritize factors contributing to the problem.

Creative Problem-Solving Techniques

1. Brainstorming and Idea Generation:
   - Divergent Thinking: Promote brainstorming sessions to generate a wide range of ideas and potential solutions without immediate judgment or criticism.
   - Mind Mapping: Introduce mind mapping techniques to visually organize thoughts, ideas, and connections related to the problem-solving process.

2. Design Thinking and Innovation:

The Wisdom of Discernment

Navigating Life's Good and Bad

- User-Centered Approach: Discuss the principles of design thinking, focusing on understanding user needs, ideating solutions, prototyping, and iterating based on feedback.

- Prototyping and Testing: Highlight the importance of prototyping as a way to quickly test and refine ideas before implementation, minimizing risks and maximizing effectiveness.

Implementation and Evaluation

1. Decision-Making and Action Planning:

- Evaluation Criteria: Introduce decision-making frameworks, such as SWOT analysis (Strengths, Weaknesses, Opportunities, Threats) or Cost-Benefit Analysis, to evaluate potential solutions based on criteria such as feasibility, impact, and alignment with organizational goals.

- Action Plans: Discuss the development of action plans outlining steps, responsibilities, timelines, and resources required to implement selected solutions effectively.

2. Monitoring and Adaptation:

- Continuous Improvement: Emphasize the importance of monitoring progress, gathering feedback, and making necessary adjustments to optimize solution outcomes.

- Iterative Problem-Solving: Encourage a culture of continuous learning and adaptation, where lessons learned from previous problem-solving experiences inform future approaches and strategies.

Overcoming Challenges in Problem-Solving

1. Collaboration and Stakeholder Engagement:

- Team Dynamics: Explore strategies for fostering collaboration, leveraging diverse perspectives, and engaging stakeholders to gain insights and collective support for problem-solving initiatives.

- Conflict Resolution: Provide techniques for addressing conflicts constructively, promoting open communication, and fostering resolutions that strengthen team dynamics and productivity.

2. Resilience and Persistence:

- Adaptability: Discuss the importance of resilience in navigating setbacks, overcoming obstacles, and maintaining motivation throughout the problem-solving process.

- Learning from Failure: Encourage a growth mindset where failures and setbacks are viewed as opportunities for learning, innovation, and continuous improvement.

Conclusion

Effective problem-solving is a critical skill that empowers individuals and teams to address challenges proactively, innovate solutions, and achieve meaningful outcomes. By employing systematic approaches, creative techniques, and collaborative strategies, individuals can enhance their problem-solving abilities, drive positive change, and contribute to personal and professional growth. Embrace the challenge of problem-solving, leverage diverse perspectives and innovative thinking, and commit to continuous improvement to navigate complexities, seize opportunities, and achieve success in dynamic environments.

Chapter 89: Navigating Career Transitions

Managing Career Changes

Navigating career transitions involves strategic planning, self-reflection, and proactive steps to successfully navigate changes in professional life.

1. Assessing Personal and Professional Goals:
- Self-Assessment: Encourage individuals to reflect on their skills, interests, values, and long-term career aspirations to identify suitable career paths and opportunities.
- Goal Setting: Discuss the importance of setting SMART (Specific, Measurable, Achievable, Relevant, Time-bound) goals to guide career transitions and align with personal growth objectives.

2. Researching Career Options:
- Market Research: Provide strategies for researching industries, companies, and job roles to understand trends, job market demand, and opportunities aligned with career goals.

- Networking: Highlight the role of networking in exploring career options, gaining insights from professionals in desired fields, and uncovering hidden job opportunities.

Finding Fulfillment in New Roles

1. Skills Development and Training:
   - Skill Enhancement: Discuss the value of acquiring new skills, certifications, or advanced training to strengthen qualifications and adapt to evolving industry demands.
   - Professional Development: Encourage participation in workshops, seminars, and online courses to enhance expertise and readiness for new career challenges.

2. Transitioning Effectively:
   - Onboarding and Integration: Provide tips for effective onboarding and integration into new roles or organizations, fostering positive relationships with colleagues, and understanding organizational culture.
   - Adaptability: Emphasize the importance of flexibility and adaptability in adjusting to new responsibilities, workflows, and expectations in different career environments.

Overcoming Challenges in Career Transitions

1. Managing Change and Uncertainty:
   - Resilience: Discuss strategies for building resilience, managing stress, and navigating uncertainties associated with career transitions, such as job changes or industry shifts.
   - Seeking Support: Encourage seeking mentorship, coaching, or peer support to gain guidance, insights, and encouragement during challenging career transitions.

2. Setting Long-Term Career Goals:
   - Career Planning: Guide individuals in developing a long-term career roadmap, setting milestones, and regularly evaluating progress towards achieving professional aspirations.
   - Continuous Learning: Promote a commitment to lifelong learning, staying updated with industry trends, and seizing opportunities for career advancement and personal growth.

Embracing Career Growth and Development

The Wisdom of Discernment
Navigating Life's Good and Bad

1. Personal Branding and Networking:

- Building Your Brand: Discuss strategies for cultivating a professional brand, enhancing online presence through LinkedIn or professional networks, and showcasing expertise and achievements.

- Networking Strategies: Provide tips for expanding professional networks, attending industry events, and leveraging connections to explore career opportunities and collaborations.

2. Work-Life Integration:

- Work-Life Balance: Emphasize the importance of maintaining work-life balance, prioritizing personal well-being, and integrating personal interests and passions into career pursuits for overall fulfillment.

- Time Management: Provide techniques for effective time management, setting boundaries, and optimizing productivity to achieve both professional success and personal satisfaction.

Conclusion

Navigating career transitions requires proactive planning, resilience, and a commitment to personal and professional growth. By assessing career goals, acquiring new skills, adapting to change, and leveraging support networks, individuals can successfully manage career changes and find fulfillment in new roles. Embrace the opportunities presented by career transitions, continuously learn and adapt to new challenges, and approach each career stage with confidence and determination to achieve long-term career success and personal fulfillment.

Chapter 90: Healthy Conflict

Understanding Productive Conflict

The Wisdom of Discernment
Navigating Life's Good and Bad

Healthy conflict is essential for growth, innovation, and fostering stronger relationships, both personally and professionally. It involves respectful disagreements that lead to constructive outcomes rather than destructive consequences.

1. Benefits of Productive Conflict:

- Enhanced Creativity: Discuss how differing viewpoints and ideas can spark creativity and innovation within teams and organizations.

- Improved Decision-Making: Explore how healthy debates and discussions can lead to better-informed decisions by considering diverse perspectives and alternatives.

2. Characteristics of Healthy Conflict:

- Respectful Communication: Emphasize the importance of active listening, empathy, and maintaining respect for others' opinions during disagreements.

- Focus on Issues, Not Personalities: Encourage separating the problem from the person, focusing discussions on facts and ideas rather than making it personal.

Strategies for Healthy Disagreements

1. Establishing Ground Rules:

- Setting Expectations: Discuss the importance of establishing clear ground rules for communication and conflict resolution within teams or relationships.

- Encouraging Open Dialogue: Promote an environment where individuals feel safe to express their opinions and concerns openly and honestly.

2. Active Listening and Empathy:

- Listening Skills: Provide techniques for active listening, such as paraphrasing, asking clarifying questions, and summarizing to ensure understanding.

- Empathetic Understanding: Highlight the role of empathy in conflict resolution, acknowledging and validating others' perspectives and emotions.

Conflict Resolution Techniques

1. Collaborative Problem-Solving:

The Wisdom of Discernment

Navigating Life's Good and Bad

- Win-Win Solutions: Encourage brainstorming and negotiation techniques that seek mutually beneficial outcomes, fostering collaboration rather than competition.
- Finding Common Ground: Discuss strategies for identifying shared goals or interests to build consensus and resolve disagreements effectively.

2. Managing Emotions and Reactions:

- Emotional Regulation: Provide strategies for managing emotions during conflicts, such as deep breathing, taking breaks, or using "I" statements to express feelings constructively.
- Conflict De-escalation: Explore methods for de-escalating tense situations, including finding common ground, acknowledging emotions, and reframing issues positively.

Building Resilient Relationships

1. Forging Stronger Connections:

- Trust and Respect: Emphasize the role of trust and respect in maintaining healthy relationships, even during times of disagreement or conflict.
- Conflict as a Growth Opportunity: Encourage individuals to view conflicts as opportunities for learning, growth, and strengthening relationships through effective resolution.

2. Learning from Conflict:

- Post-Conflict Reflection: Discuss the importance of reflecting on conflict experiences to identify lessons learned, areas for improvement, and opportunities for personal and professional development.
- Continuous Improvement: Promote a culture of continuous learning and adaptation, where feedback from conflicts informs future interactions and conflict resolution strategies.

Conclusion

Healthy conflict is not about avoiding disagreements but rather managing them in a constructive and respectful manner. By understanding the benefits of productive conflict, implementing effective communication strategies, and fostering collaborative problem-solving, individuals and teams can navigate conflicts more effectively, strengthen relationships, and achieve positive outcomes. Embrace conflict as a catalyst for growth, practice empathy and active listening, and approach disagreements with a mindset focused on resolution and mutual understanding to foster a culture of healthy conflict in all aspects of life.

Chapter 91: Living Authentically

Being True to Yourself

Living authentically involves aligning your actions, beliefs, and values with your true self, fostering a genuine and fulfilling life.

1. Self-Discovery and Reflection:
   - Exploring Identity: Encourage introspection and self-discovery to understand personal values, passions, strengths, and areas for growth.
   - Authenticity in Expression: Discuss the importance of expressing your true thoughts, feelings, and aspirations authentically in various aspects of life.

2. Embracing Individuality:
   - Celebrating Uniqueness: Highlight the value of embracing individuality and celebrating differences in perspectives, experiences, and identities.
   - Resisting External Pressures: Explore strategies for resisting societal expectations, peer pressure, and external influences that may detract from authenticity.

Embracing Authenticity in Life

1. Living in Alignment with Values:
   - Defining Personal Values: Guide individuals in identifying and prioritizing core values that guide decisions, actions, and relationships.
   - Integrity and Consistency: Discuss the importance of integrity and consistency in aligning behaviors and choices with personal values.

2. Cultivating Self-Acceptance:

The Wisdom of Discernment

Navigating Life's Good and Bad

- Self-Compassion: Promote self-compassion and acceptance of imperfections, encouraging individuals to embrace their whole selves without judgment.

- Authentic Relationships: Emphasize the role of authenticity in fostering genuine connections and meaningful relationships based on mutual respect and understanding.

Overcoming Challenges to Authenticity

1. Facing Fear and Vulnerability:

- Courageous Living: Discuss the courage required to embrace vulnerability, take risks, and pursue authenticity despite potential discomfort or fear of judgment.

- Embracing Growth: Encourage individuals to view challenges and setbacks as opportunities for personal growth and learning on the journey to authenticity.

2. Self-Expression and Creativity:

- Creative Outlets: Explore the role of creative expression, hobbies, and passions in nurturing authenticity and allowing for self-discovery and fulfillment.

- Authentic Living Practices: Provide practical strategies for integrating authenticity into daily life through mindful practices, self-care rituals, and meaningful pursuits.

Thriving Authentically

1. Impact and Influence:

- Authentic Leadership: Discuss the impact of authenticity on leadership effectiveness, influence, and inspiring others through genuine actions and values.

- Community and Contribution: Highlight the role of authenticity in building supportive communities and making meaningful contributions aligned with personal values and beliefs.

2. Reflection and Growth:

- Continuous Self-Reflection: Encourage ongoing self-reflection and evaluation of alignment with personal values, goals, and aspirations.

- Commitment to Authenticity: Inspire a commitment to lifelong authenticity, embracing evolving identities, and staying true to oneself amidst life's changes and challenges.

The Wisdom of Discernment
Navigating Life's Good and Bad

Conclusion

Living authentically is a journey of self-discovery, self-acceptance, and courageous self-expression. By aligning actions with personal values, embracing individuality, and cultivating genuine relationships, individuals can lead fulfilling lives grounded in authenticity. Embrace authenticity as a guiding principle, navigate challenges with resilience and self-compassion, and embark on a path of continuous growth and self-discovery to live authentically and wholeheartedly in all aspects of life.

Chapter 92: The Power of Meditation

Benefits of Regular Meditation

Meditation is a practice that offers numerous physical, mental, and emotional benefits, enhancing overall well-being and inner peace.

1. Stress Reduction and Relaxation:
   - Calming the Mind: Discuss how meditation techniques, such as focused breathing or mindfulness meditation, help reduce stress levels and promote relaxation.
   - Stress Response Management: Explore how regular meditation can improve the body's response to stress, reducing cortisol levels and promoting a sense of calm.

2. Improved Mental Clarity and Focus:
   - Enhancing Cognitive Function: Highlight studies showing how meditation improves cognitive abilities, such as attention span, memory retention, and decision-making skills.
   - Mindful Awareness: Explain how mindfulness practices during meditation cultivate present-moment awareness, reducing mental clutter and enhancing clarity of thought.

Simple Meditation Practices

1. Mindfulness Meditation:

The Wisdom of Discernment

Navigating Life's Good and Bad

- Breath Awareness: Guide individuals in focusing on their breath as a point of concentration, observing sensations without judgment, and returning to the breath when the mind wanders.

- Body Scan: Introduce the practice of systematically scanning the body for sensations, promoting relaxation and awareness of bodily states.

2. Guided Visualization:

- Imagery and Visualization: Discuss the use of guided imagery to create mental images of peaceful scenes or positive affirmations, promoting relaxation and emotional well-being.

- Goal-Oriented Visualization: Explore how visualization techniques during meditation can enhance motivation and goal-setting by mentally rehearsing desired outcomes.

Integrating Meditation into Daily Life

1. Consistency and Routine:

- Establishing a Practice: Encourage setting aside dedicated time daily for meditation, creating a consistent routine to reinforce the habit and experience long-term benefits.

- Start Small: Suggest beginning with short sessions and gradually increasing duration as comfort and familiarity with meditation techniques grow.

2. Emotional Resilience and Well-being:

- Managing Emotions: Discuss how meditation fosters emotional resilience by promoting self-awareness, regulating emotions, and cultivating a compassionate attitude towards oneself and others.

- Stress Management Tools: Provide individuals with meditation as a tool for navigating life's challenges, promoting emotional balance, and maintaining mental well-being.

Cultivating Mindful Living

1. Mindful Eating and Daily Activities:

- Savoring Moments: Encourage practicing mindfulness during daily activities such as eating, walking, or engaging in conversations, fostering present-moment awareness and appreciation.

The Wisdom of Discernment

Navigating Life's Good and Bad

- Reducing Multitasking: Highlight the benefits of single-tasking and focusing on one activity at a time to enhance mindfulness and overall productivity.

2. Spiritual Growth and Connection:
   - Deepening Spiritual Practice: Explore how meditation can deepen spiritual connections, fostering a sense of interconnectedness with oneself, others, and the universe.
   - Inner Peace and Fulfillment: Discuss the role of meditation in achieving inner peace, contentment, and a sense of purpose in life, aligning with personal values and aspirations.

Conclusion

The power of meditation lies in its ability to cultivate inner peace, promote mental clarity, and enhance overall well-being. By incorporating regular meditation practices into daily life, individuals can experience reduced stress, improved focus, and increased emotional resilience. Embrace meditation as a transformative tool for personal growth, cultivate mindfulness in everyday activities, and embark on a journey towards greater self-awareness and inner peace through the practice of meditation.

Chapter 93: Environmental Responsibility

Sustainable Living Practices

Environmental responsibility involves adopting habits and practices that promote the health of our planet and its ecosystems.

1. Reducing Carbon Footprint:
   - Energy Conservation: Discuss the importance of reducing energy consumption at home and in daily activities through practices such as using energy-efficient appliances, turning off lights when not in use, and minimizing heating and cooling.
   - Renewable Energy: Explore options for incorporating renewable energy sources like solar or wind power into everyday life to reduce reliance on fossil fuels.

2. Waste Reduction and Recycling:

- Recycling Initiatives: Highlight the benefits of recycling materials such as paper, glass, plastic, and metal to conserve resources, reduce landfill waste, and minimize environmental impact.

- Composting: Introduce composting as a method to reduce organic waste, enrich soil quality, and contribute to sustainable gardening practices.

Advocating for Environmental Stewardship

1. Community Engagement:

- Local Initiatives: Encourage involvement in community-based environmental projects such as park clean-ups, tree planting, or advocacy for green spaces and wildlife conservation.

- Educational Outreach: Promote sharing knowledge and raising awareness about environmental issues through community workshops, school programs, or social media campaigns.

2. Supporting Sustainable Practices:

- Ethical Consumerism: Discuss the role of informed consumer choices in supporting businesses and products that prioritize environmental sustainability, fair trade practices, and ethical sourcing.

- Policy Advocacy: Explore opportunities to engage in advocacy efforts for environmental policies at local, national, and international levels that promote conservation, renewable energy adoption, and biodiversity protection.

Living Responsibly

1. Water Conservation:

- Efficient Water Use: Provide tips for conserving water at home, such as fixing leaks, installing water-saving devices, and practicing mindful water consumption habits.

- Sustainable Landscaping: Discuss practices for sustainable landscaping, including native plant gardening, rainwater harvesting, and using eco-friendly lawn care products.

2. Personal Commitment:

- Lifestyle Choices: Encourage individuals to make environmentally conscious choices in transportation, food consumption, and travel to reduce their ecological footprint.

- Continuous Learning: Emphasize the importance of staying informed about current environmental issues, scientific research, and technological innovations that support sustainable living practices.

Promoting Long-term Sustainability

1. Corporate Responsibility:
- Business Ethics: Highlight the role of businesses and corporations in adopting sustainable practices, reducing greenhouse gas emissions, and implementing eco-friendly policies.
- Supply Chain Transparency: Advocate for transparency in supply chains, promoting ethical sourcing, and minimizing environmental impact throughout the production and distribution process.

2. Personal Impact:
- Individual Contribution: Discuss how individual actions collectively contribute to global efforts in combating climate change, preserving natural resources, and protecting biodiversity.
- Inspiring Others: Encourage leading by example and inspiring others to embrace environmental responsibility through personal actions, advocacy, and community leadership.

Conclusion

Environmental responsibility is a collective commitment to safeguarding our planet for future generations. By adopting sustainable living practices, advocating for environmental stewardship, and promoting long-term sustainability in personal, community, and global contexts, individuals can contribute to a healthier and more resilient planet. Embrace environmental responsibility as a fundamental value, take proactive steps to reduce environmental impact, and empower others to join in creating a sustainable future for all.

Chapter 94: The Art of Negotiation

The Wisdom of Discernment

Navigating Life's Good and Bad

Negotiation Techniques

Negotiation is a skillful process of reaching agreements or compromises while navigating differences and achieving mutually beneficial outcomes.

1. Preparation and Strategy:
   - Setting Objectives: Discuss the importance of defining goals and priorities before entering negotiations to clarify desired outcomes.
   - Research and Information Gathering: Explore strategies for gathering relevant information about the other party, market conditions, and alternative options to strengthen negotiation positions.

2. Effective Communication:
   - Active Listening: Highlight the role of active listening in understanding the other party's concerns, interests, and underlying needs during negotiations.
   - Clear and Concise Communication: Provide techniques for expressing ideas, proposals, and concerns clearly and concisely to facilitate mutual understanding and avoid misunderstandings.

Achieving Win-Win Outcomes

1. Collaborative Problem-Solving:
   - Identifying Common Ground: Encourage finding areas of agreement and shared interests to build trust and foster a collaborative negotiation environment.
   - Creative Solutions: Explore techniques such as brainstorming or exploring multiple options to generate creative solutions that meet the needs of both parties.

2. Building Relationships:
   - Building Trust: Discuss the importance of trust-building behaviors, such as honesty, reliability, and transparency, in establishing productive and sustainable negotiation relationships.

- Long-term Perspective: Emphasize the value of considering long-term implications and maintaining positive relationships beyond the current negotiation for future collaborations.

Handling Challenges

1. Managing Emotions and Pressure:
 - Emotional Intelligence: Provide strategies for managing emotions effectively, maintaining composure, and responding calmly to emotional triggers during negotiations.
 - Handling Conflict: Discuss techniques for resolving conflicts constructively and de-escalating tense situations to keep negotiations on track.

2. Flexibility and Adaptability:
 - Adapting to Change: Encourage flexibility in adjusting negotiation strategies based on new information, evolving priorities, or unexpected developments.
 - Win-Win Mindset: Promote a win-win mindset focused on achieving mutual benefits and preserving relationships, even in complex or challenging negotiations.

Ethical Considerations

1. Integrity and Fairness:
 - Ethical Standards: Highlight the importance of upholding ethical standards, fairness, and integrity throughout the negotiation process to build credibility and trust.
 - Respect for Differences: Discuss the value of respecting cultural, ethical, and personal differences to foster inclusive and respectful negotiations.

Continuous Improvement

1. Reflecting and Learning:
 - Post-Negotiation Analysis: Encourage reflecting on negotiation outcomes, identifying lessons learned, and areas for improvement in future negotiations.
 - Professional Development: Advocate for continuous learning and development of negotiation skills through workshops, courses, and mentorship opportunities.

Conclusion

The art of negotiation combines strategic planning, effective communication, collaborative problem-solving, and ethical considerations to achieve win-win outcomes and build sustainable relationships. By mastering negotiation techniques, embracing a win-win mindset, and continuously improving negotiation skills, individuals can navigate differences, resolve conflicts, and achieve mutually beneficial agreements in various personal, professional, and societal contexts. Embrace negotiation as a valuable skill, hone your negotiation prowess, and approach each negotiation opportunity as a chance to create value and foster positive outcomes for all parties involved.

Chapter 95: Building Community

Engaging with Local Communities

Building community involves fostering connections and creating a sense of belonging among individuals within a local or broader community setting.

1. Active Participation:
  - Community Involvement: Discuss the importance of actively participating in community events, volunteer initiatives, and local organizations to contribute positively to community life.
  - Supporting Local Businesses: Encourage supporting local businesses and enterprises to promote economic growth and community resilience.

2. Collaborative Projects:
  - Collaborative Problem-Solving: Highlight the benefits of collaborative efforts in addressing community challenges, such as environmental issues, infrastructure improvements, or social services.
  - Shared Resources: Explore opportunities for sharing resources, knowledge, and skills within the community to enhance collective well-being and capacity-building.

Creating a Sense of Belonging

The Wisdom of Discernment
Navigating Life's Good and Bad

1. Inclusivity and Diversity:

   - Celebrating Diversity: Emphasize the value of embracing cultural, ethnic, and socioeconomic diversity within the community to foster inclusivity and mutual respect.

   - Creating Safe Spaces: Discuss the importance of creating safe and welcoming environments where all community members feel accepted and valued.

2. Communication and Connection:

   - Open Communication: Advocate for transparent communication channels and platforms that facilitate dialogue, information-sharing, and collaboration among community members.

   - Social Bonds: Highlight the significance of social interactions, neighborhood gatherings, and shared experiences in strengthening social bonds and fostering a sense of belonging.

Building Resilient Communities

1. Empowerment and Leadership:

   - Empowering Individuals: Encourage individuals to take on leadership roles, initiate grassroots projects, and advocate for community needs and priorities.

   - Capacity Building: Promote opportunities for skill-building, training, and mentorship to empower community members to actively participate in community development efforts.

2. Long-term Sustainability:

   - Environmental Stewardship: Discuss strategies for promoting sustainable practices, conservation efforts, and environmental awareness within the community.

   - Resilience Planning: Explore resilience planning initiatives, such as disaster preparedness, emergency response strategies, and community resilience-building workshops.

Nurturing Community Spirit

1. Cultural and Arts Initiatives:

   - Promoting Arts and Culture: Highlight the role of arts, cultural events, and creative expressions in nurturing community identity, pride, and cohesion.

The Wisdom of Discernment
Navigating Life's Good and Bad

- Community Celebrations: Encourage organizing festivals, community celebrations, and cultural heritage events to foster unity and celebrate shared values.

2. Generational Connections:
   - Inter-generational Activities: Advocate for inter-generational programs and activities that bridge age gaps, promote mentorship, and preserve community traditions.
   - Youth Engagement: Empower youth through leadership opportunities, educational programs, and youth-led initiatives that contribute to community growth and vitality.

Conclusion

Building community is a collaborative endeavor that thrives on active participation, inclusivity, and a shared commitment to fostering connections and creating a sense of belonging. By engaging with local communities, celebrating diversity, promoting resilience, and nurturing community spirit through collaborative projects and shared experiences, individuals can contribute to building vibrant, resilient, and thriving communities. Embrace community-building as a journey of connection, empowerment, and collective action toward creating inclusive, supportive, and sustainable environments for all community members.

Chapter 96: Storytelling for Impact

Crafting Compelling Stories

Storytelling is a powerful tool for communicating ideas, inspiring action, and connecting with audiences on an emotional level.

1. Structuring Your Story:
   - Beginning, Middle, End: Discuss the importance of a clear narrative structure with a captivating beginning, a compelling middle that builds tension or intrigue, and a satisfying resolution.
   - Character Development: Explore techniques for developing relatable characters that resonate with your audience and drive the narrative forward.

2. Emotional Appeal:

  - Eliciting Emotions: Highlight the role of emotions in storytelling, such as empathy, excitement, or hope, to engage listeners and evoke a memorable response.

  - Authenticity and Vulnerability: Encourage authenticity and vulnerability in storytelling to build trust and establish a genuine connection with your audience.

Using Storytelling to Inspire and Influence

1. Creating Impactful Messages:

  - Clarity and Purpose: Emphasize the importance of a clear message or takeaway that aligns with your goals, whether it's to inspire, educate, or advocate for change.

  - Call to Action: Discuss strategies for incorporating a compelling call to action that motivates listeners to take meaningful steps or make informed decisions based on your story.

2. Visual and Verbal Techniques:

  - Visual Storytelling: Explore the use of visuals, such as imagery, videos, or slides, to enhance storytelling and create a multi-sensory experience for your audience.

  - Voice and Tone: Discuss the significance of voice modulation, pacing, and tone in delivering your story with impact, emphasizing key moments and maintaining audience engagement.

Leveraging Storytelling Across Contexts

1. Professional Settings:

  - Business Narratives: Provide examples of how storytelling can be used in business settings, such as pitching ideas, presenting data, or influencing stakeholders.

  - Leadership Communication: Explore how leaders can use storytelling to articulate vision, motivate teams, and build a cohesive organizational culture.

2. Personal Narratives:

  - Personal Branding: Discuss how storytelling can enhance personal branding efforts by showcasing your unique experiences, values, and strengths.

- Networking and Relationships: Highlight the role of storytelling in forming connections, building rapport, and leaving a lasting impression in personal and professional relationships.

Ethical Considerations

1. Authenticity and Truthfulness:
  - Factual Accuracy: Stress the importance of maintaining factual accuracy and truthfulness in storytelling to uphold credibility and trust with your audience.
  - Respecting Privacy: Discuss ethical considerations when sharing personal or sensitive stories, respecting privacy boundaries, and obtaining consent where necessary.

Continuous Improvement

1. Feedback and Reflection:
  - Receiving Feedback: Encourage seeking constructive feedback on your storytelling techniques to refine your narrative style and effectiveness.
  - Self-Reflection: Promote regular self-reflection on your storytelling experiences, identifying strengths, areas for improvement, and opportunities for growth.

Conclusion

Storytelling is a dynamic and versatile skill that can be used to create impact, inspire change, and foster meaningful connections across various contexts. By crafting compelling stories with emotional appeal, clarity of message, and authenticity, individuals can leverage storytelling to inspire and influence others, drive positive outcomes, and make a lasting impact in professional, personal, and community settings. Embrace storytelling as a transformative tool for communication, advocacy, and personal expression, harnessing its power to connect with audiences, ignite change, and shape a brighter future.

Chapter 97: Overcoming Limiting Beliefs

Identifying and Challenging Limiting Beliefs

The Wisdom of Discernment
Navigating Life's Good and Bad

Limiting beliefs are negative thoughts or assumptions that hold you back from reaching your full potential.

1. Recognizing Limiting Beliefs:
  - Self-awareness: Discuss the importance of self-awareness in identifying recurring negative thoughts or beliefs that undermine your confidence and progress.
  - Common Examples: Provide examples of common limiting beliefs, such as "I'm not good enough," "I don't deserve success," or "I'll never be able to..."

2. Challenging Negative Thought Patterns:
  - Evidence and Rationality: Encourage examining the evidence supporting these beliefs and questioning their rationality or validity.
  - Cognitive Restructuring: Introduce techniques like cognitive restructuring, where you actively replace negative thoughts with more realistic and empowering beliefs.

Replacing Them with Empowering Beliefs

1. Affirming Positive Statements:
  - Positive Affirmations: Explore the use of positive affirmations to counteract limiting beliefs and reinforce new, empowering beliefs about yourself and your abilities.
  - Visualization: Discuss visualization techniques where you imagine yourself succeeding and embodying the qualities of your new empowering beliefs.

2. Building Self-Confidence:
  - Skill Development: Highlight the role of skill development and continuous learning in boosting self-confidence and reinforcing positive beliefs.
  - Past Successes: Encourage reflecting on past achievements and successes to build evidence supporting your new empowering beliefs.

Implementing Changes

1. Behavioral Changes:

- Taking Action: Emphasize the importance of taking small, manageable steps towards your goals despite initial doubts or fears associated with limiting beliefs.

- Accountability: Discuss the benefits of accountability partners or support networks in providing encouragement and reinforcement during your journey.

2. Embracing Growth Mindset:

- Embracing Challenges: Advocate for embracing challenges as opportunities for growth and learning, rather than reinforcing limiting beliefs.

- Learning from Setbacks: Encourage resilience and learning from setbacks as part of the process of overcoming and replacing limiting beliefs.

Sustaining Progress

1. Mindfulness and Reflection:

- Mindfulness Practices: Introduce mindfulness techniques to observe and manage negative thought patterns as they arise, promoting greater self-awareness and emotional regulation.

- Regular Reflection: Promote regular reflection on your progress, celebrating milestones and identifying areas for further growth in maintaining empowering beliefs.

Conclusion

Overcoming limiting beliefs is a transformative journey of self-discovery and personal growth. By identifying, challenging, and replacing negative thought patterns with empowering beliefs, individuals can unlock their full potential, cultivate resilience, and achieve greater fulfillment in personal and professional endeavors. Embrace the process of self-awareness, positive affirmation, and continuous learning as essential tools in overcoming limiting beliefs, empowering yourself to pursue your goals with confidence, clarity, and determination.

Chapter 98: Pursuing Lifelong Passions

Keeping Passions Alive Throughout Life

The Wisdom of Discernment

Navigating Life's Good and Bad

Passions are the driving forces that bring joy, purpose, and fulfillment to our lives, regardless of age or circumstances.

1. Identifying Your Passions:

  - Self-Exploration: Encourage self-reflection and exploration to identify activities and interests that ignite your enthusiasm and bring you joy.

  - Early Influences: Discuss how childhood interests and experiences can provide clues to lifelong passions that endure over time.

2. Nurturing Your Passions:

  - Making Time: Emphasize the importance of prioritizing and dedicating time to engage in activities that nurture your passions regularly.

  - Continuous Learning: Highlight the role of continuous learning and skill development in deepening your understanding and enjoyment of your passions.

Balancing Passion with Responsibility

1. Integration into Daily Life:

  - Finding Balance: Discuss strategies for integrating your passions into your daily routine while managing responsibilities such as work, family, and other obligations.

  - Setting Boundaries: Explore the importance of setting boundaries and prioritizing activities that align with your passions to maintain a healthy balance.

2. Personal Growth and Fulfillment:

  - Emotional Well-being: Highlight how pursuing passions contributes to emotional well-being, reducing stress, and increasing overall life satisfaction.

  - Achieving Goals: Discuss setting goals related to your passions and the sense of accomplishment and fulfillment that comes from working towards and achieving them.

Conclusion

Pursuing lifelong passions is not only a source of joy and fulfillment but also contributes to personal growth, resilience, and well-being throughout life. By identifying and nurturing your

The Wisdom of Discernment

Navigating Life's Good and Bad

passions, and finding ways to integrate them into your daily life while maintaining a healthy balance with responsibilities, you can cultivate a sense of purpose and happiness that enriches every aspect of your life journey. Embrace your passions with enthusiasm, dedication, and a commitment to lifelong learning and growth, ensuring that they continue to inspire and fulfill you in the years to come.

Chapter 99: Creating a Legacy

Planning Your Legacy

Creating a legacy involves intentionally shaping the impact you leave on others and the world, reflecting your values, accomplishments, and contributions.

1. Defining Your Values and Vision:
   - Reflecting on Values: Encourage introspection to identify core values that guide your life and will define your legacy.
   - Vision for Impact: Discuss envisioning the impact you want to have on future generations, communities, or causes.

2. Setting Goals for Your Legacy:
   - Long-term Goals: Outline specific goals and milestones that align with your vision for creating a meaningful legacy.
   - Short-term Actions: Break down long-term goals into actionable steps that can be taken in the present to move closer to your desired legacy.

Taking Steps to Build a Lasting Impact

1. Personal Contributions:
   - Sharing Knowledge and Skills: Discuss ways to share your expertise, experiences, and wisdom with others through mentoring, teaching, or writing.
   - Philanthropy and Giving: Explore opportunities for philanthropic activities or charitable giving that support causes you care about and contribute to your legacy.

2. Building Relationships:

   - Connecting with Others: Highlight the importance of building meaningful relationships with family, friends, colleagues, and community members as part of your legacy.

   - Networking for Impact: Discuss networking strategically to amplify your influence and reach in areas related to your legacy goals.

Embracing Challenges and Growth

1. Adapting to Change:

   - Flexibility and Resilience: Encourage embracing challenges and setbacks as opportunities for growth and adaptation in shaping your legacy.

   - Learning from Failures: Discuss the role of resilience and learning from failures or setbacks as part of the journey toward creating a lasting impact.

2. Reflection and Adjustment:

   - Continuous Evaluation: Promote regular reflection on progress toward your legacy goals, adjusting strategies as needed to stay aligned with your vision.

   - Seeking Feedback: Encourage seeking feedback from trusted individuals to gain perspective and refine your approach to building a lasting legacy.

Conclusion

Creating a legacy is a deliberate and ongoing process that involves aligning your values, vision, and actions to leave a positive impact on future generations and communities. By defining your values, setting clear goals, and taking intentional steps to contribute to causes you care about, you can build a meaningful legacy that reflects your values, passions, and aspirations. Embrace challenges as opportunities for growth, cultivate relationships, and continuously adapt your approach to leave a lasting and meaningful impact that resonates far beyond your lifetime.

Chapter 100: Conclusion: The Journey of Discernment

Reflecting on the Journey

The Wisdom of Discernment
Navigating Life's Good and Bad

The journey of discernment is a transformative process of self-discovery, personal growth, and understanding that enables individuals to distinguish between good and bad, make informed decisions, and navigate life's complexities with clarity and wisdom.

1. Personal Growth and Development:
  - Self-awareness: Reflecting on personal strengths, weaknesses, values, and beliefs that shape perspectives, decisions, and interactions with others.
  - Emotional Intelligence: Cultivating emotional intelligence, empathy, and self-regulation to understand and manage emotions, relationships, and interpersonal dynamics effectively.

2. Acquiring Wisdom and Insight:
  - Critical Thinking: Developing critical thinking skills to analyze information, evaluate evidence, and make reasoned judgments in various contexts and situations.
  - Discernment: Honing discernment skills to assess situations, identify patterns, and make sound decisions aligned with personal values, ethics, and principles.

Moving Forward with Wisdom

Moving forward with wisdom involves applying lessons learned, embracing continuous growth, and integrating discernment into daily life to foster resilience, purpose, and fulfillment.

1. Integrating Discernment into Decision-Making:
  - Decision-Making: Applying discernment principles to navigate ethical dilemmas, challenges, and opportunities with integrity, clarity, and foresight.
  - Risk Management: Assessing risks, consequences, and potential outcomes to make informed choices that align with long-term goals, aspirations, and values.

2. Contributing to Positive Change and Impact:
  - Social Responsibility: Engaging in civic engagement, advocacy, or philanthropy to promote social justice, equity, and sustainable development in communities and society.

The Wisdom of Discernment
Navigating Life's Good and Bad

- Leadership: Exercising ethical leadership, influence, and responsibility to inspire others, foster collaboration, and drive positive change in organizations and beyond.

3. Continued Learning and Growth:
- Lifelong Learning: Embracing lifelong learning, curiosity, and open-mindedness to adapt to change, expand knowledge, and innovate in personal and professional endeavors.
- Personal Fulfillment: Pursuing passions, interests, and meaningful experiences that nurture personal growth, happiness, and overall well-being.

By reflecting on the journey of discernment, integrating wisdom into decision-making processes, and committing to lifelong learning and growth, individuals can cultivate resilience, foster positive relationships, and lead purposeful lives grounded in values, integrity, and continuous self-improvement. This concluding chapter encourages readers to embrace discernment as a lifelong journey of personal transformation, empowerment, and contribution to a more informed, compassionate, and just world.

The Wisdom of Discernment

Navigating Life's Good and Bad

Thank you to all the readers of this book on discernment. Your dedication to exploring and understanding the principles of identifying good versus bad, and recognizing the intentions behind actions, is commendable. Through this journey of discernment, may you continue to grow in wisdom, make informed choices, and contribute positively to your lives and the lives of those around you.

Your engagement and commitment to personal development and ethical decision-making are essential in creating a more thoughtful and compassionate world. May the insights gained from this book empower you to navigate life's complexities with clarity, integrity, and resilience.

Wishing you continued success and fulfillment on your journey of discernment.

Sincerely,

CR 2009/2024

Angel Viera, Author